AF623832

# MILESTONES

Sayyid Qutb

KITAB BHAVAN
Publishers, Distributors, Exporters & Importers

**KITAB BHAVAN**
Publishers, Distributors, Exporters & Importers
1784, Kalan Mahal, Darya Ganj,
New Delhi - 1100 02 (India)

Phones : (91-11)23277392/93,23274686
Fax : (91-11)23263383

Online Store: www.kitabbhavan.net

Email : info@kitabbhavan.net
: nasri@vsnl.com

Book Code No. : M00020

ISBN : *978-81-9335-731-6*

***Printed & Published in India by :***
Nusrat Ali Nasri for KITAB BHAVAN
Moonis Ali Nasri for KITAB BHAVAN
1784, Kalan Mahal, Darya Ganj,
New Delhi-1100 02 [India]

*In the name of Allah,*
*Most Gracious, Most merciful*

# INTRODUCTION

Islam stands for change. It seeks to change the individual and the society. This change covers every aspect of human life, from personal morality to business, economics, and politics. It is only natural that Islam should be fought by those who oppose change. This is the way it has been throughout history. It happened to Noah, Abraham, Moses, Jesus, and Muhammad (Peace be on them). It will happen to anyone who wants to stand up and proclaim the true message of Islam to the world today. Sayyid Qutb, the author of this book, tried to bring together some of the fine points of Islam and Islamic work in the present volume. It seems that true Islamic principles are too much for the corrupt regimes of the self — proclaimed leaders of so — called Islamic countries. Sayyid Qutb was persecuted, and eventually hanged. The ultimate price for working to please God Almighty and to propagate his ways in this world is often one's own life. The author tried to do it; he paid for it with his life. If you and I try to do it, there is every likelihood we will be called upon to do the same. But for those who truly believe in God, what other choice is there?

# CONTENTS

# BIOGRAPHY

Ash-Shaheed (the Martyr) Sayyid Qutb, who some thirty years after his death is still the most influential ideologue of the as-Sahwah (Islamic revival) in the contemporary Muslim world, began life in the obscurity of the village of Musha (or Qaha) near Asyut in Upper Egypt. He was born there in 1906 to a father who was well regarded in the village for his zuhd (piety) and ilm (learning). He was the eldest of five children and was followed by a brother, Muhammad Qutb, also destined to gain fame as a prolific writer and da'yee (caller to Islam). His sisters, Amina and Hamida, came to attain some prominence in the ranks of the Ikhwan (Muslim Brotherhood).

Encouraged by both his parents, Sayyid Qutb swiftly developed a love for learning, and by the age of ten he had become a hafidh (memorizer) of the Qur'an at the local primary school. Three years later, the family moved to Helwan, enabling him to enter the preparatory school for the Dar al-Ulum in Cairo - a prestigious teachers training college which he joined in 1929.

### *Early Career*

On graduating in 1933, he was appointed to teach at the Dar al-Ulum, and a few years later entered the service of the Egyptian Ministry of Education. The year 1933 also saw the beginning of Sayyid Qutb's extraordinarily varied and prolific literary career. His first book was Muhimmat al-Sha'irf 'l-Hayah (The Task of the Poet in Life), and for more than a decade literature remained together with education his principal preoccupation. He wrote poetry, autobiographical sketches, works of literary criticism, and novels and short stories dealing with the problems of love and marriage. Later he came to repudiate much of this early work and publicly distanced himself from his own writings.

Sayyid Qutb was an active member of the oppositional Wafd party, and he became a prominent critic of the Egyptian monarchy. This brought him into inevitable conflict with his superiors at the Ministry of Education, and it took the efforts of Taha Hussain to dissuade him from resigning. Sayyid Qutb sought anew, in 1947, to emancipate himself from government employment by becoming editor-in-chief of two journals, al- 'Alam al-'Arabi (The Arab

World) and al-Fikr al-Jadid (New Thought). He lost his position with the former as a result of editorial disagreements, and the latter which sought to present the model of an Islamic society free of corruption, tyranny, and foreign domination, was banned after only six issues. While continuing to write for a wide range of literary and political periodicals, ash-shaheed Sayyid Qutb stayed in the Ministry of Education.

### *Impressions of America*

In 1948, the Ministry sent him on a study mission to the United States, doubtless with the assumption that direct acquaintance with America would incline him more favourably to official policies and induce him to abandon the oppositional activities that were increasingly taking on an Islamic dimension.

Sayyid Qutb's impressions of America were, however, largely negative. While noting American achievements in production and social organization, Sayyid Qutb laid heavy emphasis on materialism, racism, and sexual permissiveness as dominant features of American life. 'It is astonishing to realize, despite his advanced education and his perfectionism, how primitive the American really is in his views on life...His behaviour reminds us of the era of the 'caveman'. He is primitive in the way he lusts after power, ignoring ideals and manners and principles...It is difficult to differentiate between a church and any other place that is set up for entertainment, or what they call in their language, fun,'

His sojourn in the United States coincided, moreover, with the first Palestine war, and he noted with dismay the uncritical acceptance of Zionist ideals by American public opinion and the ubiquity of anti-Islamic prejudice. After completing a master's degree in education at the University of Northern Colourado in Greeley, ash-shaheed Sayyid Qutb decided to forego the possibility of staying in America to earn a doctorate and returned to Egypt in 1951.

### *Return to Egypt*

For his part, Sayyid Qutb had been increasingly well disposed to the Ikhwan ul Muslimeen (Muslim Brotherhood) ever since he witnessed the ecstatic reception given in America to the news of the assassination, on February 12 1949, of Imam Hasan al-Banna, founder of the organization. His perception of the Ikhwan as defenders of Islam was further strengthened after his return to Egypt when a British official, James Heyworth Dunne, told him that the Ikhwan represented the only barrier to the establishment of 'Western civilization' in the Middle East.

Sayyid Qutb's joined the Ikhwan ul Muslimeen (Muslim Brotherhood) almost immediately after his return from America and in 1953 became the editor-inchief of 'al-Ikhwan al-Muslimun,' the Brotherhood's official journal.

On July 23, 1952, the Egyptian monarchy was overthrown in a coup d'etat mounted by a group of soldiers who styled themselves the 'Free Officers'. They were formally led by General Muhammad Najib (aka Naguib), but it soon became apparent that Jamal Abdul Nasir (aka Nasser) was the driving force behind the group. Although originally welcomed by the Ikhwan, it became obvious that the revolution was being led by the Revolutionary Command Council (R.C.C.) towards a secular state rather an Islamic one.[3] On July 26, three days after the revolution, the Ikhwan publicly announced that the R.C.C. must establish the Shari'ah (Islamic law) as the basis of Egypt.

On July 19 1954, the R.C.C. concluded an agreement with Great Britain which meant that British forces would retreat from the Suez Canal in exchange for Egypt's co-operation for British commercial interests. The Ikhwan outright rejected the treaty and denounced it as 'treason' to Islam.

### *Sentenced to Fifteen Years Imprisonment*

The R.C.C. decreed the dissolution of the Muslim Brotherhood and arrested the leaders of the Ikhwan, including Sayyid Qutb, along with 4,000 members, many of whom were given sentences of life imprisonment.[4] Ash-shaheed Sayyid Qutb had a high fever when he was arrested, but the state-security officers handcuffed him and took him to prison. He fainted several times on the way. For several hours, he was kept in a cell with vicious dogs, and then, during long periods of interrogation, he was beaten. His trial was overseen by three judges, one of whom was a future President of Egypt, Anwar Sadat. In the courtroom, Sayyid Qutb ripped off his shirt to display the marks of torture.

He was sentenced to fifteen years imprisonment and was now destined to spend the rest of his life in prison, with the exception of eight short months of relative liberty in 1965.

Inhumane treatment and torture was used regularly in interrogating members of the Ikhwan. Zainab al-Ghazali, one of Ikhwan's leading female members, recalls in her memoirs, 'the door was locked and a bright light switched on....the room was full of dogs! I could not count how many!

---

3 Derkmejian, R.H., Egypt under Nasir, p. 25.
4 Derkmejian, R.H., Egypt under Nasir, p. 27.

Scared, I closed my eyes and put my hands to my chest.

Within seconds the snarling dogs were all over me, I could feel their teeth tearing into every part of my body...the dogs were unrelenting, digging their teeth into my scalp, my shoulders, back, chest and wherever another had not already taken hold.'[5]

The ordeal of imprisonment has been a common, almost universal experience for Ulema (scholars) and Du'at (callers) in the modern world. For many of them, it has meant not only suffering, but also the opportunity to reflect on past struggles, to review theories and strategies, to deepen and sharpen their insight, to plan and reorganize.

### *In Prison*

Western writers in recent years have focused on ash-shaheed Sayyid Qutb as one of the two most influential Muslim thinkers of the 20th century, the other being Maulana Mawdudi. In prison, ash-shaheed Sayyid Qutb was introduced to Maulana Mawdudi's ideas, especially his emphasis on Islam being a complete way of life and the establishment of the Shari'ah (Islamic law) on earth as every Muslim's primary responsibility.

While in jail, ash-shaheed Sayyid Qutb was also able to complete a number of his most important writings including the Qur'anic commentary Fi Zilal al-Qur an (In the Shade of the Qur'an). His tafsir (exegesis) has been acclaimed as one of the best contemporary tafsir of the Qur'an in any language and one that has passed through several editions and reprints.

Professor Muhammed Qutb (Sayyid's brother) writes, '(In the Shade of the Qur'an) is the fruit of the most productive years of its author's (Sayyid Qutb's) intellectual life, and at the same time, a vivid expression of the sacred battle which he fought and which culminated in his martyrdom in 1966.'6 Prof. Muhammed Qutb further notes that if one reads the Qur'an in a sort of passive, detached state one is sure to miss a lot of its indications and purposes. But when one reads it while actually involved in the cause trying to establish 'la ilaha illallah' (There is no deity worthy of worship except Allah), one's heart will open to receive its meanings which would otherwise have missed, and will draw interferences of which one was totally unaware. 'In the Shade of the Qur'an' is a proof of this fact.

Clearly inspired by the circumstances of daily struggle and confrontation in which he lived, ash-shaheed Sayyid Qutb concludes, 'To live 'In the

5 Al-Ghazali, Z., Return of the Pharaoh, p.50.

6 Qutb, M., Foreword: In the Shade of the Qur'an, p.xi

Shade of the Qur'an' is a great blessing which only can be fully appreciated by those who experience it. It is a rich experience that gives meaning to life and makes it worth living.'[7]

Along with writing his exegesis of the Qur'an, ash-shaheed Sayyid Qutb also dedicated some time in writing poetry. His most famous poem is entitled 'From Behind Bars' which begins with the following verses:

My brother, you are free behind these gates.
My brother, you are free within these chains.
For if upon Allah you do rely.
The intrigues of his slaves can bring no pains

### 'Jahilliyah'

The savagery and torture ash-shaheed Sayyid Qutb and other inmates suffered over the years, including the massacre of twenty-one members of the Ikhwan at the Liman Tura military jail in June 1957, forced him to conclude that a regime unprecedented in its ruthlessness had come to power in Egypt and that the primary problem was no longer overt foreign rule or the absence of social justice. It was rather the total usurpation of power by forces intensely hostile to Islam, with the result that the entire life of society was fixed in the non-Islamic patterns into which it had gradually fallen as a result of decay and neglect.

Sayyid Qutb concluded that the Egyptian government along with all other governments in the Muslim world were strictly comparable to pre-Islamic Arabia in its ignorance and disregard for divine precepts and that its state could therefore rightly be designated by the same term - Jahiliyyahh. Occurring four times in the Qur'an, the term Jahiliyyahh assumed central significance for Sayyid Qutb, encapsulating the utter bleakness of the Muslim predicament and serving as an epistemological device for rejecting all allegiances other than Islam.

According to Sayyid Qutb, this new Jahiliyyahh had deep historical roots, and it was moreover fostered and protected by all the coercive apparatus of a modern, authoritarian state; it could not, therefore, be easily remedied in the short term.

What was needed was a long-term program of ideological and organizational work, coupled with the training of a dedicated vanguard of believers who would protect the cause in times of extreme danger (if

7 Qutb, S., Introduction: In the Shade of the Qur'an, p.xvii.

necessary by recourse to force) and preside over the replacement of Jahiliyyahh by the Islamic state.

Sayyid Qutb first developed these ideas in dialogue with a small number of his fellow inmates, and then included them in notes that were smuggled out of jail to be read by members of his family and others close to them. These notes then became the basis of his most prolific book, Ma`alim fi Tariq (Milestones). The leader of Ikhwan at the time, Murshid al-Hudaybi said, 'with Allah Almighty's grace, this book (Milestones) has confirmed all my trust in Sayyid, may Allah preserve him. Sayyid, God willing, is now the awaited hope for da'wah.'[8]

It began to be circulated underground in manuscript form for a couple of years before being published in Cairo where it was quickly banned. Consequently anyone caught with a copy would be charged with sedition. In its final form 'Milestones' consisted of some of the letters ash-shaheed Sayyid Qutb had sent from prison and key sections of Fi Zilal al-Qur'an. It represented a concise and forceful summary of the main ideas Sayyid Qutb had developed: the Jahilli nature of existing society, government, and culture, and the long-term program needed for the establishment of an Islamic state.

Ash-shaheed Sayyid Qutb writes in 'Milestones', 'Mankind today is on the brink of a precipice. Humanity is threatened not only by nuclear annihilation but by the absence of values. The West has lost its vitality and Marxism has failed. At this crucial and bewildering juncture, the turn of Islam and the Muslim community has arrived.'

Continuously read and reprinted down to the present, and translated into most languages, 'Milestones' is arguably the most important Islamic literary piece written in the 20th century.

### *Released and Re-arrested*

In December 1964, Sayyid Qutb was released from jail. It is said that his release was due in part to continuing ill health and in part to the intercession of Abdul Salam Arif, the president of Iraq, who invited him to settle in his country. Given the tragic denouncement to this last period of relative freedom in the life of Sayyid Qutb, it is however, possible that the Egyptian government set him free in order to create the conditions for his re-arrest, trial, and final elimination.

Although accused of a conspiracy, he was in fact the victim of one.

---

8 Al-Ghazali, Z., Return of the Pharaoh, p.40.

On August 5, 1965, Sayyid Qutb was rearrested; two weeks later, his sisters Amina and Hamida were also arrested, together with Zaynab al-Ghazali, the leading female member of the Ikhwan. Sayyid Qutb was accused of subversion and terrorism and the encouragement of sedition. The first charge rested only on the fact that, in 1959, he had been entrusted by Murshid al-Hudaybi with responsibility for organizing the Ikhwan in the jails and prison camps of Egypt. This organization, known as the Tanzim, was supposedly linked to the circles studying his prison letters and dedicated to the immediate and bloody overthrow of the Egyptian government. No evidence was presented in court to show that Sayyid Qutb or any group linked to him was plotting armed insurrection, and Sayyid Qutb was even able to establish that on two occasions he had dissuaded members of the Ikhwan from attempting such activity, not least because the needed change, by its very nature, had to be brought about by popular action.

In support of the second charge, the encouragement of sedition, the prosecution placed great emphasis on Milestones, and it became apparent that this book, with its proven widespread appeal and long-term revolutionary implications, represented the crux of the Egyptian government's concern. So on May 17, 1966, the court condemned ash-shaheed Sayyid Qutb to death, together with six other prominent members of the Muslim Brotherhood, including al-Hudaybi.

Ash-shaheed Sayyid Qutb received the death sentence by saying, 'Alhamdullilah (all praise is for Allah) I performed Jihad for fifteen years until I earned this Shahadah (martyrdom).'

### *Sentenced to Death*

Sayyid Qutb anticipated his end before the sentence was issued welcomed it and did not accept any attempts to change his stance until his end came because this, he felt, was how his words would truly impact the masses. He writes 'Indeed our words will remain lifeless, barren, devoid of any passion, until we die as a result of these words, whereupon our words will suddenly spring to life and live on amongst the hearts that are dead, bringing them back to life as well...'[9] He would tell his fellow inmates, 'Brother(s) push ahead, for your path is soaked in blood. Do not turn your head right or left but look only up to Heaven.'[10]

The journalist Mahmud ar-Rakaabi narrated a strange discussion that took place between himself and ash-shaheed Sayyid Qutb at his house

9 Qutb, S., Milestones.

10 Zhawahiri, Sh., Dr., A., Knights under the Prophets Banner, al-Sharq al-Aswat.

before his imprisonment. Ar-Rakaabi recalls, "I said to him, 'Praise be to Allah upon well-being - whatever Allah wills - your health is good, all you need now is a bride?' So Sayyid laughed very much and said, 'Which bride are you referring to [in this world or the next?]' I said, 'We were created for both of them.' So we spoke for a while, then he suddenly asks me, 'Can you interpret dreams? For I had a vision last night that a red snake wrapped itself around me and then tightened itself on me. Then I woke up that hour and couldn't go back to sleep. I said, 'My sir! That's a gift, to be presented to you by one of the believers, wrapped with a red ribbon, and if you wish I will present it to you now, so take it and continue with your sleep.' He said, 'Why can't the interpretation of the dream be that I am the gift presented to the believers?' I said, 'Isn't the existence of the righteous more beneficial for the Islamic Da'wah? He said, 'Not always. In fact, sometimes their departure is more beneficial! Although, I am not intending my own destruction, but we must intend firmness in our stance, knowing that the firmness in stance can bring about destruction.'

I said, 'O Man! Don't be pessimistic like that, for people should aim to be balanced in everything.' He said: 'You will come to know." [11]

Many offers were made to ash-shaheed Sayyid Qutb in order that he abandon his views and declare himself free from the Ikhwan. He was requested to write a mere line or a sentence to President Abdul Nasir seeking his pardon which would lead to him being released from the prison, the death sentence alleviated and the world opened up to him, for him to take from it what he liked from positions in government to incalculable amounts of wealth. Yet ash-shaheed Sayyid Qutb completely rejected any attempts made to make him deviate from his beliefs in return for removing his death sentence.

Such attempts at bargaining continued until the last night of his life when the Egyptian government used his sister Hameedah to pressurise him to respond to her request. She says, 'Hamzah al-Basyuni - the Prison Officer - called me to his office, and showed me the death sentence and the signature on it. Then he said to me that the government would be ready to alleviate the sentence if my brother were to respond to their request. He said to me, 'Surely, your brother is a loss to the entire Egypt, and not you alone. I cannot imagine losing this person after a few hours. We want to save him from execution, by any way and by any means. Only a few words need he utter to save himself from execution, and no one can have the same influence over him as yourself, and you alone can be

11 Fareed, A., Mawaaqif Imaaniyah, p. 265, Dar Taybah ed.3.

responsible for saying this to him. Whilst I am responsible for informing him about this, there is no one better than you to inform him of this matter. He need only say a few words, and that will be the end of the matter. We want him to say: this movement (Ikhwan) has connections with such and such front... After that, the matter has ended, as far as you are concerned, and as for him, then he would be pardoned due to health reasons!'

I said to him, 'But you know as Abdul Nasir knows that this movement has no connections with any front.' Hamzah al-Basyuni said, 'I know, and we all know that you are the only front in Egypt that works for the sake of Aqeedah. We know that you are the best of people in the country, but we want to rescue Sayyid Qutb from execution.' So he looked at Safwat ar-Rubi and said, 'Take her - O Safwat - to her brother.'

So I went to my brother and informed him of what they wanted from him. He looked at me to see the expression on my face, as if he were saying - Are you requesting this, or is it them? I managed to convey to him through my actions that it was them. Then he looked at me and said, 'By Allah! If this speech was true, I would have surely said it! No power on the face of this earth would be able to prevent me from saying this. But it didn't happen, and I would never tell a lie.' Safwat asked him, 'Meaning, this is your opinion?' Sayyid answered, 'Yes!' Then Safwat left us saying, 'Anyhow, sit with each other for a while.'

Then I informed him of the story from the beginning, and said to him, 'Hamzah al-Basyuni called me and showed me the death sentence, and asked me to request this of you.' He asked me, 'Are you pleased with it?' I said, 'No'. He said 'They cannot harm or benefit themselves. Indeed, the span of one's life is in the Hands of Allah. They are not able to prolong a life span or shorten it, for all of that is in the Hands of Allah, and Allah is all encompassing their affairs.'[12]

Ash-shaheed Sayyid Qutb uttered many expressions in the air of bargaining and persuasion, rejecting all efforts to shake him from his stance and to abandon his Aqeedah (beliefs). One of his inmates asked him, 'Why were you so open in the court that holds your neck under its threat?' He replied, 'Because concealment is not permissible in 'Aqeedah, and it is not for the leader to take the allowances in religion.'

One of his most infamous sayings was uttered when he was asked to write a few words seeking pardon from Abdul Nasir. He said: 'Verily, the index finger that testifies to the oneness of Allah in prayer, utterly rejects to

12 Fareed, A., Mawaaqif Imaaniyah, p. 265, Dar Taybah ed.3.

write even a letter, endorsing the rule of the Taghout (tyrant).' And, 'Why should I seek his pardon? If I have been imprisoned rightfully, then I accept the right judgement, and if I have been imprisoned falsely, then I am greater than having to seek pardon from falsehood.'

### *Sayyid Qutb is Martyred*

Generally prisoners would not know when they are due to be executed because of public sensitivities. Consequently, the date of the execution of Sayyid Qutb was kept hidden even from Qutb himself. On the day of his execution the military officer entered Sayyid Qutb's cell under the pretext that he has been ordered to change his cell quarters. However ash-shaheed Sayyid Qutb knew that this was not just another cell change and said, 'I know where you are taking me, for the Prophet Muhammed T ccame to me in my dream and told me (about today), so take me. '

After many attempts by politicians and scholars to intercede on his behalf, including King Faisal[13] and Ibn Baz,[14] ash-shaheed Sayyid Qutb was hurriedly hanged on August 29th 1966, together with two of his companions, Muhammad Yusuf Awwash[15] and Abdul Fattah Isma'il.

Zainab al-Ghazali recalls hearing the news in her prison cell with Sayyid Qutb's sister, Hamidah, 'we heard that the death sentences on Imam Shaheed Sayyid Qutb (along with the others)...had been carried out. News of the executions fell on us like a dead weight, for those executed were all dear, good Mujahids. How was I to console Sayyid's sister?...Rather, how was I to console myself and find comfort in all this calamity?.....Such a great loss. Sayyid Qutb, the Mufassir (exegete) of the Qur'an and Islamic Da'iyah (caller), a sage in his understanding, eloquence, clarity and force of argument. A man who held fast to his religion, trusting in Allah's victory...Words do not console at the time of such events!

Read Milestones to find out why Sayyid was executed! Sayyid Qutb even forecast Islamic resurgence in the lands of both superpowers. That meant the end of these superpowers, one day, and the establishment of the rule of Islam in order to abolish Jahilli anarchy. Indeed, the rise of Islam means the establishment of the only legal power which has the right to govern the world.'[16]

---

13 Fareed, A., Mawaaqif Imaaniyah, p. 265, Dar Taybah ed.3.

14 Refer to Appendix VI: Fatwah by Shaykh Ibn Jibreen.

15 Refer to Appendix III: An Interview with the wife of Yusuf Awwash.

16 Al-Ghazali, Z., Return of the Pharaoh, p.165/6.

On the day of ash-Shaheed Sayyid Qutb's execution, Zainab al-Ghazali saw Sayyid Qutb in a dream; he told her, 'Know that I was not with them, I was in Madina in the company of the Prophet T'. The following day Zainab had another dream,

'I..dozed after Fajr prayer while reading the supplication of the concluding prayer, and heard a voice saying, 'Sayyid is in the highest (Jannat) Firdous (highest part of Paradise)'. I woke and related the same to Hamidah who cried, saying 'I am sure of Allah's favour on us and that, God willing, Sayyid in the highest Firdous...these visions are consolation, a strengthening from Allah, the Exalted, the High' [17]

The Nasser regime thought that the Islamic movement 'received a deadly blow with the execution of Sayyid Qutb and his companions - but the apparent surface calm concealed an immediate interaction with Sayyid Qutb's ideas and the formation of the nucleus of the modern Islamic Jihad movement in Egypt.'[18]

* * *

17 Al-Ghazali, Z., Return of the Pharaoh, p.166.

18 Zhawahiri, Dr., A., Knights under the Prophets Banner, al-Sharq al-Aswat, December 2001.

### *Sources/Bibliography*

o Abdo, G., No God But God, Oxford University Press.

o Bangash, Z., Remembering Sayyid Qutb, an Islamic Intellectual and leader of rare insight and integrity, Institute of Contemporary Thought, - App. I, Milestones, Maktabah, 2005.

o Dekmejian, R.H., Islam in Revolution: Fundamentalism in the Arab World, Syracuse University Press, New York, 1986.

- Egypt under Nasir, SUNY Press, 1971.

o Faraj, A.S., Absent Obligation, Maktabah Publications, Birmingham, 2000.

o Al-Ghazali, Z., Return of the Pharaoh, Islamic Foundation, Leicester, 1994

o Hadad, Y.Y., The Qur'anic Justification For An Islamic Revolution: The View of Sayyid Qutb, The Middle East Journal, vol. 37, 1983, pp. 14-31.

-.Sayyid Qutb: Ideologue of Islamic Revival, ed. John L. Esposito, Voices of Resurgent Islam, Oxford University Press, New York, 1983.

o Hiro, D., Islamic Fundamentalism, Paladin Press, 1988.

o Husaini, I.M., The Moslem Brethren, Khayat, Lebanon, 1956.

o Johns, A.H., Let My People Go! Sayyid Qutb and the Vocation of Moses, Islam and Christian-Muslim Relations Journal, vol. 1-2, 1991, pp. 139-170.

o Katab, S., al-Hudaybi's Influence on the Development of Islamist Movements in Egypt, The Muslim World, vol. 91, no.3, 2001, pp. 451-479.

o El-Kadi, A., Sayyid Qutb, www.youngmuslims.ca/biographies/display.asp?ID=7

o Kerpat, K.H., Political and Social Thought in Contemporary Middle East, Praeger Press, 1982.

o Khadduri, M., Political Trends in the Arab World, The Role of Ideas and Ideals in Politics, The Johns Hopkins Press, Maryland, 1972.

o Mousalli, A.S., Radical Islamic Fundamentalism: The Ideological and Political Discourse of Sayyid Qutb, American University of Beirut, 1995.

o Mitchell, R.D., The Society of Muslim Brothers, Oxford University Press, 1969.

o Munson, H., Islam and Revolution in the Middle East, Yale University

Press, 1988.

- Naguib, M., Egypt's Destiny, Victor Collancz, London, 1995.
- Qutb, S., Milestones, Maktabah Booksellers and Publishers, Birmingham, 2005.

  - Social Justice in Islam, Islamic Book Trust, Kuala Lumpur, 2000.

  - In the shade of the Qur'an - Fee Zilale Qur'an, Islamic Foundation, 2001.
- Ramadan, Fundamentalist Influence in Egypt, in Fundamentalism Comprehended, ed. Martin Marty and Scott Appleby, University of Chicago Press, 1995.
- Rubin, B., Islamic Fundamentalism in Egyptian Politics, Macmillan, 1990.
- Saddiqui, K., Issues in the Islamic Movement, The Open Press, 1985.
- Shadid, A., Legacy of the Prophet, Despots, Democrats, and the New Politics of Islam, Westview Press, 2000.
- Shepard, W.E., Sayyid Qutb and Islamic Activism: A Translation and Critical Analysis of Social Justice in Islam, Brill, Leiden, 1996.
- Taylor, A.R., The Islamic Question in the Middle East Politics, Westview Press, 1988.
- Zayyat, M., The Road to al-Qaeda, Pluto Press, 2004.
- Zhawahiri, Sh., Dr. A., Knights under the Prophets Banner, al-Sharq al-Aswat, December 2001.

# AUTHOR'S PREFACE

Mankind today is on the brink of a precipice, not because of the danger of complete annihilation which is hanging over its head — this being just a symptom and not the real disease — but because humanity is devoid of those vital values which are necessary not only for its healthy development but also for its real progress. Even the Western world realises that Western civilization is unable to present any healthy values for the guidance of mankind. It knows that it does not possess anything which will satisfy its own conscience and justify its existence.

Democracy in the West has become infertile to such an extent that it is borrowing from the systems of the Eastern bloc, especially in the economic system, under the name of socialism. It is the same with the Eastern bloc. Its social theories, foremost among which is Marxism, in the beginning attracted not only a large number of people from the East but also from the West, as it was a way of life based on a creed. But now Marxism is defeated on the plane of thought, and if it is stated that not a single nation in the world is truly Marxist, it will not be an exaggeration. On the whole this theory conflicts with man's nature and its needs. This ideology prospers only in a degenerate society or in a society which has become cowed as a result of some form of prolonged dictatorship. But now, even under these circumstances, its materialistic economic system is failing, although this was the only foundation on which its structure was based. Russia, which is the leader of the communist countries, is itself suffering from shortages of food. Although during the times of the Tsars Russia used to produce surplus food, it now has to import food from abroad and has to sell its reserves of gold for this purpose. The main reason for this is the failure of the system of collective farming, or, one can say, the failure of a system which is against human nature.

It is essential for mankind to have new leadership!

The leadership of mankind by Western man is now on the decline, not because Western culture has become poor materially or because its economic and military power has become weak. The period of the Western system has come to an end primarily because it is deprived of those life — giving values which enabled it to be the leader of mankind.

It is necessary for the new leadership to preserve and develop the material fruits of the creative genius of Europe, and also to provide mankind with such high ideals and values as have so far remained undiscovered by mankind, and which will also acquaint humanity with a way of life which is harmonious with human nature, which is positive and constructive, and which is practicable.

Islam is the only system which possesses these values and this way of life.

The period of the resurgence of science has also come to an end. This period, which began with the Renaissance in the sixteenth century after Christ and reached its zenith in the eighteenth and nineteenth centuries, does not possess a reviving spirit.

All nationalistic and chauvinistic ideologies which have appeared in modern times, and all the movements and theories derived from them, have also lost their vitality. In short, all man — made individual or collective theories have proved to be failures.

At this crucial and bewildering juncture, the turn of Islam and the Muslim community has arrived — the turn of Islam, which does not prohibit material inventions. Indeed, it counts it as an obligation on man from the very beginning of time, when God deputed him as His representative on earth, and regards it under certain conditions as worship of God and one of the purposes of man's creation.

وَإِذْ قَالَ رَبُّكَ لِلْمَلَٰٓئِكَةِ إِنِّي جَاعِلٌ فِي ٱلْأَرْضِ خَلِيفَةً

***"And when Your Sustainer said to the angels, 'I am going to make My representative on earth.,"***

***(Qur'an 2:30)***

وَمَا خَلَقْتُ ٱلْجِنَّ وَٱلْإِنسَ إِلَّا لِيَعْبُدُونِ ﴿٥٦﴾

***"And I have not created jinns and men except that they worship Me." (51:56)***

Thus the turn of the Muslim community has come to fulfill the task for mankind which God has enjoined upon it.

كُنتُمْ خَيْرَ أُمَّةٍ أُخْرِجَتْ لِلنَّاسِ تَأْمُرُونَ بِٱلْمَعْرُوفِ
وَتَنْهَوْنَ عَنِ ٱلْمُنكَرِ وَتُؤْمِنُونَ بِٱللَّهِ

***"You are the best community raised for the good of mankind. You enjoin what is good and forbid what is wrong, and you believe in God." (3:110)***

وَكَذٰلِكَ جَعَلْنٰكُمْ اُمَّةً وَّسَطًا لِّتَكُوْنُوْا شُهَدَآءَ عَلَى النَّاسِ
وَيَكُوْنَ الرَّسُوْلُ عَلَيْكُمْ شَهِيْدًا ؕ

***"Thus We have made you a middle community, so that you be witnesses for mankind as the Messenger is a witness for you." (2:143)***

* * *

Islam cannot fulfill its role except by taking concrete form in a society, rather, in a nation; for man does not listen, especially in this age, to an abstract theory which is not seen materialized in a living society. From this point of view, we can say that the Muslim community has been extinct for a few centuries, for this Muslim community does not denote the name of a land in which Islam resides, nor is it a people whose forefathers lived under the Islamic system at some earlier time. It is the name of a group of people whose manners, ideas and concepts, rules and regulations, values and criteria, are all derived from the Islamic source. The Muslim community with these characteristics vanished at the moment the laws of God became suspended on earth.

If Islam is again to play the role of the leader of mankind, then it is necessary that the Muslim community be restored to its original form.

It is necessary to revive that Muslim community which is buried under the debris of the man — made traditions of several generations, and which is crushed under the weight of those false laws and customs which are not even remotely related to the Islamic teachings, and which, in spite of all this, calls itself the 'world of Islam.'

I am aware that between the attempt at 'revival' and the attainment of 'leadership' there is a great distance, as the Muslim community has long ago vanished from existence and from observation, and the leadership of mankind has long since passed to other ideologies and other nations, other concepts and other systems. This was the era during which Europe's genius created its marvellous works in science, culture, law and material production, due to which mankind has progressed to great heights of creativity and material comfort. It is not easy to find fault with the inventors of such marvellous things, especially since what we call the 'world of Islam' is completely devoid of all this beauty.

But in spite of all this, it is necessary to revive Islam. The distance between the revival of Islam and the attainment of world leadership may be vast, and there may be great difficulties on the way; but the first step must be taken for the revival of Islam.

* * *

If we are to perform our task with insight and wisdom, we must first know clearly the nature of those qualities on the basis of which the Muslim community can fulfill its obligation as the leader of the world. This is essential so that we may not commit any blunders at the very first stage of its reconstruction and revival.

The Muslim community today is neither capable of nor required to present before mankind great genius in material inventions, which will make the world bow its head before its supremacy and thus re — establish once more its world leadership.

Europe's creative mind is far ahead in this area, and at least for a few centuries to come we cannot expect to compete with Europe and attain supremacy over it in these fields.

Hence we must have some other quality, that quality which modern civilization does not possess.

But this does not mean that we should neglect material progress. We should also give our full attention and effort in this direction, not because at this stage it is an essential requirement for attaining the leadership of mankind, but because it is an essential condition for our very existence; and Islam itself, which elevates man to the position of representative of God on earth, and which, under certain conditions, considers the responsibilities of this representative as the worship of God and the purpose of man's creation, makes material progress obligatory for us.

To attain the leadership of mankind, we must have something to offer besides material progress, and this other quality can only be a faith and a way of life which on the one hand conserves the benefits of modern science and technology, and on the other fulfills the basic human needs on the same level of excellence as technology has fulfilled them in the sphere of material comfort. And then this faith and way of life must take concrete form in a human society — in other words, in a Muslim society.

* * *

If we look at the sources and foundations of modern ways of living, it becomes clear that the whole world is steeped in ***Jahiliyyah***,[1] and all the marvellous material comforts and high — level inventions do not diminish this ignorance. This ***Jahiliyyah*** is based on rebellion against God's sovereignty on earth. It transfers to man one of the greatest attributes of God, namely sovereignty, and makes some men lords over others. It is now not in that simple and primitive form of the ancient ***Jahiliyyah*** , but takes the form of claiming that the right to create values, to legislate rules of collective behaviour, and to choose any way of life rests with men, without regard to what God has prescribed. The result of this rebellion against the authority of God is the oppression of His creatures. Thus the humiliation of the common man under the communist systems and the exploitation of individuals and nations due to greed for wealth and imperialism under the capitalist systems are but a corollary of rebellion against God's authority and the denial of the dignity of man given to him by God.

In this respect, Islam's way of life is unique, for in systems other that Islam, some people worship others in some form or another. Only in the Islamic way of life do all men become free from the servitude of some men to others and devote themselves to the worship of God alone, deriving guidance from Him alone, and bowing before Him alone.

This is where the roads separate, and this is that new concept which we possess and can present to mankind — this and the way of life which this concept organizes for all the practical aspects of man's life. This is that vital message of which mankind does not know. It is not a product of Western invention nor of European genius, whether eastern or western.

* * *

Without doubt, we possess this new thing which is perfect to the highest degree, a thing which mankind does not know about and is not capable of 'producing'.

But as we have stated before, the beauty of this new system cannot be appreciated unless it takes a concrete form. Hence it is essential that a community arrange its affairs according to it and show it to the world. In order to bring this about, we need to initiate the movement of Islamic revival in some Muslim country. Only such a revivalist movement will eventually attain to the status of world leadership, whether the distance is near or far.

How is it possible to start the task of reviving Islam? It is necessary that there should be a vanguard which sets out with this determination and then keeps walking on the path, marching through the vast ocean of ***Jahiliyyah***

---

1. Ignorance of the Divine guidance.

which has encompassed the entire world. During its course, it should keep itself somewhat aloof from this all — encompassing ***Jahiliyyah*** and should also keep some ties with it.

It is necessary that this vanguard should know the landmarks and the milestones of the road toward this goal so that they may recognize the starting place, the nature, the responsibilities and the ultimate purpose of this long journey. Not only this, but they ought to be aware of their position as opposed to this ***Jahiliyyah***,which has struck its stakes throughout the earth: when to co — operate with others and when to separate from them: what characteristics and qualities they should cultivate, and with what characteristics and qualities the ***Jahiliyyah*** immediately surrounding them is armed; how to address the people of ***Jahiliyyah*** in the language of Islam, and what topics and problems ought to be discussed; and where and how to obtain guidance in all these matters.

The milestones will necessarily be determined by the light of the first source of this faith — the Holy Qur'an — and from its basic teachings, and from the concept which it created in the minds of the first group of Muslims, those whom God raised to fulfill His will, those who once changed the course of human history in the direction ordained by God.

* * *

I have written **"*Milestones*"** for this vanguard, which I consider to be a waiting reality about to be materialized. Four chapters[2] are taken from my commentary, ***Fi Thilal al-Qur'an***,[3] which I have changed here and there slightly to suit the topic. This introduction and the other chapters I wrote at various times. In writing these chapters I have set down the deep truths which I grasped during my meditations over the way of life presented in the Holy Qur'an. These thoughts may appear random and disconnected, but one thing is common among them; that is, these thoughts are milestones on the road,' and it is the nature of signs along the road to be disconnected. Taken together, these writings are a first installment of a series, and with God's help I hope to write some more collections on this topic.

And the guidance is from God.

---

2. These chapters are "The Nature of the Qur'anic Method". "Islamic Concept and Culture", "**Jihaad** in the Cause of God", and "Revival of the Muslim Community and its characteristics.
3. **In the Shades of the Qur'an**, a commentary on the Qur'an.

## CHAPTER 1

# THE UNIQUE QUR'ANIC GENERATION

The callers to Islam in every country and in every period should give thought to one particular aspect of the history of Islam, and they should ponder over it deeply. This is related to the method of inviting people to Islam and its ways of training.

At one time this Message created a generation — the generation of the Companions of the Prophet, may God be pleased with them — without comparison in the history of Islam, even in the entire history of man. After this, no other generation of this calibre was ever gain to be found. It is true that we do find some individuals of this calibre here and there in history, but never again did a great number of such people exist in one region as was the case during the first period of Islam.

This is an obvious and open truth of history, and we ought to ponder over it deeply so that we may reach its secret.

The Qur'an of this Message is still in our hands, and the Hadith of the Messenger of God — peace be on him, i.e. his guidance in practical affairs, and the history of his sacred life are also in our hands, as they were in the hands of the first Muslim community whose equal history could not produce again. The only difference is the person of the Messenger of God — peace be on him; but is this the secret?

Had the person of the Prophet — peace be on him — been absolutely essential for the establishment and fruition of this message, God would not have made Islam a universal message, ordained it as the religion for the whole of mankind, given it the status of the last Divine Message for humanity, and made it to be a guide for all the inhabitants of this planet in all their affairs until the end of time.

God has taken the responsibility for preserving the Holy Qur'an on Himself because He knows that Islam can be established and can benefit mankind even after the time of the Prophet — peace be on him. Hence He called His Prophet — peace be on him — back to His mercy after twenty three years of messengership and declared this religion to be valid until the end of time. Therefore the absence of the Messenger of God — peace be on him — is not the real cause for, nor does it explain, this phenomenon.

We look, therefore, for some other reasons, and for this purpose we look at that clear spring from which the first generation of Muslims quenched their thirst. Perhaps something has been mixed with that clear spring. We should look at the manner in which they received their training. Perhaps some changes have found their way into it.

The spring from which the Companions of the Prophet — peace be on him — drank was the Qur'an; only the Qur'an as the Hadith of the Prophet and his teachings were offspring of this fountainhead. When someone asked the Mother of the Faithful, 'Aisha — may God be pleased with her, — about the character of the Prophet — peace be on him, — she answered, "His character was the Qur'an"[4]

The Holy Qur'an was the only source from which they quenched their thirst, and this was the only moud in which they formed their lives. This was the only guidance for them, not because there was no civilization or culture or science or books or schools. Indeed, there was Roman culture, its civilization, its books and its laws, which even today are considered to be the foundation of European culture. There was the heritage of Greek culture — its logic, its philosophy and its arts, which are still a source of inspiration for Western thought.

There was the Persian civilization, its art, its poetry and its legends, and its religion and system of government. There were many other civilizations, near or far, such as the Indian and Chinese cultures, and so on. The Roman and Persian cultures were established to the north and to the south of the Arabian peninsula, while the Jews and Christians were settled in the heart of Arabia. Thus we believe that this generation did not place sole reliance on the Book of God for the understanding of their religion because of any ignorance of civilization and culture, but it was all according to a well thought out plan and method. An example of this purpose is found in the displeasure expressed by the Messenger of God — peace be on him — when 'Umar — may God be pleased with him — brought some pages from the Torah. The Messenger of God — peace be on him — said, "By God, if even Moses had been alive among you today, he would have no recourse except to follow me"[5]

---

4. Al-Nisaa
5. Reported by al-Hafidh Abu Yala-from Himad, from al-Shubi, from Jabir.

It is clear from this incident that the Messenger of God — peace be on him — deliberately limited the first generation of Muslims, which was undergoing the initial stages of training, to only one source of guidance, and that was the Book of God. His intention was that this group should dedicate itself purely to the Book of God and arrange its lives solely according to its teachings. That is why the Messenger of God — peace be on him — was displeased when 'Umar — may God be pleased with him — turned to a source different from th'e Qur'an.

In fact, the Messenger of God — peace be on him — intended to prepare a generation pure in heart, pure in mind, pure in understanding. Their training was to be based on the method prescribed by God Who gave the Qur'an, purified from the influence of all other sources.

This generation, then, drank solely from this spring and thus attained a unique distinction in history. In later times it happened that other sources mingled with it. Other sources used by later generations included Greek philosophy and logic, ancient Persian legends and their ideas, Jewish scriptures and traditions, Christian theology, and, in addition to these, fragments of other religions and civilizations. These mingled with the commentaries on the Qur'an and with scholastic theology, as they were mingled with jurisprudence and its principles. Later generations after this generation obtained their training from this mixed source, and hence the like of this generation never arose again.

Thus we can say without any reservations that the main reason for the difference between the first unique and distinguished group of Muslims and later Muslims is that the purity of the first source of Islamic guidance was mixed with various other sources, as we have indicated.

* * *

There is another basic cause which has operated in creating this difference. That difference is in the method of learning of this unique generation.

They of the first generation did not approach the Qur'an for the purpose of acquiring culture and information, nor for the purpose of taste or enjoyment. None of them came to the Qur'an to increase his sum total of knowledge for the sake of knowledge itself or to solve some scientific or legal problems, or to remove some defect in his understanding. He rather turned to the Qur'an to find out what the Almighty Creator had prescribed for him and for the group in which he lived, for his life and for the life of the group. He approached it to act on what he heard immediately, as a soldier on the battlefield reads "Today's Bulletin" so that he may know what is to be done. He did not read many verses of the Qur'an in one session, as he understood that this would lay an unbearable burden of duties and responsibilities on his shoulders. At most he would read ten verses, memorize them, and then act upon them. We know this from a tradition reported by Abdullah bin Mas'ood .

This understanding — the understanding that instruction is for action — opened the doors to spiritual fulfillment and to knowledge. If they had read the Qur'an only for the sake of discussion, learning and information, these doors would not have opened. Moreover, action became easy, the weight of responsibilities became light, and the Qur'an became a part of their personalities, mingling with their lives and characters so that they became living examples of faith — a faith not hidden in intellects or books, but expressing itself in a dynamic movement which changed conditions and events and the course of life.

Indeed, this Qur'an does not open its treasures except to him who accepts it with this spirit: the spirit of knowing with the intention of acting upon it. It did not come to be a book of intellectual content, or a book of literature, or to be considered as a book of stories or history, although it has all these facets. It came to become a way of life, a way dedicated to God. Thus, God Most High imparted it to them in a gradual manner, to be read at intervals:

وَقُرْآنًا فَرَقْنَاهُ لِتَقْرَأَهُ عَلَى النَّاسِ عَلَىٰ مُكْثٍ وَنَزَّلْنَاهُ تَنْزِيلًا ﴿١٠٦﴾

***"We have revealed this Qur'an little by little so that you may recite it to people at intervals, and We have revealed it gradually." (17:106)***

The Qur'an did not come down all at once; rather it came down according to the needs of the Islamic society in facing new problems, according to the growth of ideas and concepts, according to the progress of general social life, and according to new challenges faced by the Muslim community in its practical life. One verse or a few verses would be revealed according to the special circumstances and events, and they would answer questions which arose in the minds of people, would explain the nature of a particular situation, and would prescribe a way of dealing with it. These verses would correct their mistakes, either of understanding or of practice, would bring them closer to God, and would explain to them the wisdom of the various aspects of the universe in the light of God's attributes. Thus they clearly realized that every moment of their lives was under the continuous guidance and direction of the Almighty Creator and that they were traversing the path of life under the wings of God's mercy. Because of this sense of constant relationship with God, their lives were moulded according to that sacred way of life which was being instructed by Him.

Thus, instruction to be translated into action was the method of the first group of Muslims. The method of later generations was instruction for academic discussion and enjoyment. And without doubt this is the second major factor which made later generations different from the first unique generation of Islam.

* * *

A third cause is also operative in the history of Muslims; we ought to look at it also. When a person embraced Islam during the time of the Prophet — peace be on him — he would immediately cut himself off from ***Jahiliyyah***.[6] When he stepped into the circle of Islam, he would start a new life, separating himself completely from his past life under ignorance of the Divine Law. He would look upon the deeds during his life of ignorance with mistrust and fear, with a feeling that these were impure and could not be tolerated in Islam! With this feeling, he would turn toward Islam for new guidance; and if at any time temptations overpowered him, or the old habits attracted him, or if he became lax in carrying out the injunctions of Islam, he would become restless with a sense of guilt and would feel the need to purify himself of what had happened, and would turn to the Qur'an to mould himself according to its guidance.

Thus, there would be a break between the Muslim's present Islam and his past ***Jahiliyyah***, and this after a well thought out decision, as a result of which all his relationships with ***Jahiliyyah*** would be cut off and he would be joined completely to Islam, although there would be some give — and — take with the polytheists in commercial activity and daily business; yet relationships of understanding are one thing and daily business is something else.

This renunciation of the ***jahili*** environment, its customs and traditions, its ideas and concepts, proceeded from the replacement of polytheism by the concept of the Oneness of God, of the ***jahili*** view of life and the world by that of the Islamic view, and from absorption into the new Islamic community under a new leadership and dedication of all loyalties and commitments to this new society and new leadership.

This was the parting of the ways and the starting of a new journey, a journey free from the pressures of the values, concepts and traditions of the ***jahili*** society. The Muslim encountered nothing burdensome except

---

6. The state of ignorance of the guidance from God.

the torture and oppression; but he had already decided in the depths of his heart that he would face it with equanimity, and hence no pressure from the ***jahili*** society would have any effect on his continuing steadfastness.

We are also surrounded by ***Jahiliyyah*** today, which is of the same nature as it was during the first period of Islam, perhaps a little deeper. Our whole environment, people's beliefs and ideas, habits and art, rules and laws — is ***Jahiliyyah***, even to the extent that what we consider to be Islamic culture, Islamic sources, Islamic philosophy and Islamic thought are also constructs of ***Jahiliyyah***!

This is why the true Islamic values never enter our hearts, why our minds are never illuminated by Islamic concepts, and why no group of people arises among us who are of the calibre of the first generation of Islam.

It is therefore necessary — in the way of the Islamic movement — that in the early stages of our training and education we should remove ourselves from all the influences of the ***Jahiliyyah*** in which we live and from which we derive benefits. We must return to that pure source from which those people derived their guidance,the source which is free from any mixing or pollution.

We must return to it to derive from it our concepts of the nature of the universe, the nature of human existence, and the relationship of these two with the Perfect, the Real Being, God Most High. From it we must also derive our concepts of life, our principles of government, politics, economics and all other aspects of life.

We must return to it with a sense of instruction for obedience and action, and not for academic discussion and enjoyment. We should return to it to find out what kind of person it asks us to be, and then be like that. During this process, we will also discover the artistic beauty in the Qur'an, the marvellous tales in the Qur'an, the scenes of the Day of Judgment in the Qur'an, the intuitive logic the Qur'an, and all other such benefits which are sought in the Qur'an by academic and literary people. We will enjoy all these other aspects, but these are not the main object of our study. Our primary purpose is to know what way of life is demanded of us by the Qur'an, the total view of the universe which the Qur'an wants us to have, what is the nature of our knowledge of God taught to us by the Qur'an, the kind of morals and manners which are enjoined by it, and the kind of legal and constitutional system it asks us to establish in the world.

We must also free ourselves from the clutches of ***jahili*** society, ***jahili*** concepts, ***jahili*** traditions and ***jahili*** leadership. Our mission is not to compromise with the practices of ***jahili*** society, nor can we be loyal to it. ***Jahili*** society, because of its ***jahili*** characteristics, is not worthy to be compromised with. Our aim is first to change ourselves so that we may later change the society.

Our foremost objective is to change the practices of this society. Our aim is to change the ***jahili*** system at its very roots — this system which is fundamentally at variance with Islam and which, with the help of force and oppression, is keeping us from living the sort of life which is demanded by our Creator.

Our first step will be to raise ourselves above the ***jahili*** society and all its values and concepts. We will not change our own values and concepts either more or less to make a bargain with this ***jahili*** society. Never! We and it are on different roads, and if we take even one step in its company, we will lose our goal entirely and lose our way as well. We know that in this we will have difficulties and trials, and we will have to make great sacrifices. But if we are to walk in the footsteps of the first generation of Muslims, through whom God established His system and gave it victory over ***Jahiliyyah***, then we will not be masters of our own wills.

It is therefore desirable that we should be aware at all times of the nature of our course of action, of the nature of our position, and the nature of the road which we must traverse to come out of ignorance, as the distinguished and unique generation of the Companions of the Prophet — peace be on him — came out of it.

## CHAPTER 2

# THE NATURE OF THE QUR'ANIC METHOD

The Meccan portion of the holy Qur'an, revealed to the Prophet — peace be on him — over a period of thirteen years, dealt with only one question. The nature of this question did not change, although the manner of its presentation varied according to the style of the Qur'an, which refers to this question in new ways, always as though it had been raised for the first time.

This was the primary question, the greatest question, the fundamental question of this new religion — a question of faith with two main aspects, the Divine and the human, and the relationship between them.

This question is addressed to 'the human being' as a human being, and in this respect the Arab of one era or any other, and the non — Arab, are equal, whether he belongs to that time or to later times.

This is that human problem which does not change; this is the question of man's existence in the universe, his ultimate goal, and his position and relationship to the universe; and the question of the relationship between him and the Creator of the universe. This aspect of man's life cannot change, as it relates to his very being.

During the Meccan period, the Qur'an explained to man the secret of his existence and the secret of the universe surrounding him. It told him who he is, where he has come from, for what purpose and where he will go in the end, Who brought him from nonexistence into being, to Whom he will return, and what his final disposition will be. It also informed him concerning the nature of the things which he can touch and see and the things which he can sense and conceive but which he cannot see, Who created and administers this marvellous universe, Who alternates night and day, and Who renovates and varies things. It also told him how to relate to the Creator, to the physical world, and to other human beings.

This is that great question upon which man's existence depends and will continue to depend until the end of time.

And thus the full thirteen years of the Meccan period were spent in explaining and expounding this fundamental question, that question from which all other questions and details pertaining to human life are derived.

The Qur'an made this question the only subject of its message during the Meccan period and never discussed other subsidiary and derived matters. These subsidiary topics were not mentioned until the All — Knowing God decided that matters pertaining to faith had been explained fully and had entered into the hearts of that select group of people who were to establish His religion and were to give it a practical form.

* * *

Those who call toward God's Religion and want to establish the way of life prescribed by this Religion should ponder at length over this significant fact, that for thirteen years the Qur'an exclusively expounded this faith and did not deviate from this issue to describe the details of that system which was to be established on this faith or any laws for the organization of the Muslim society.

It was God's wisdom that this fundamental question of faith and belief should be made the central theme of the initial call of the Prophet to his people. The first message which the Messenger of God — peace be on him — brought to these people was that they bear witness that "there is no deity except God" and he devoted his efforts to making known to people Who their true Sustainer is and that they should worship Him alone.

From the viewpoint of the limited understanding of man, it does not seem as though this would be the easiest way to reach the hearts of the Arabs. They knew their language well and knew the meaning of '**Ilah**' (god), and they also knew the meaning of '**La ilaha illa Allah**' (There is no deity except God). They knew that '**Uluhiyah**' means 'sovereignty,' and they also realized that ascribing sovereignty only to God meant that the authority would be taken away from the priests, the leaders of tribes, the wealthy and the rulers, and would revert to God. It meant that only God's authority would prevail in the heart and conscience, in matters pertaining to religious observances and in the affairs of life such as business, the distribution of wealth and the dispensation of justice — in short, in the souls and bodies of men. They knew very well that the proclamation, "there is no deity except 'Allah,' was a challenge to that worldly authority which had usurped the greatest attribute of God, namely, sovereignty. It was a rebellion against all modes of behaviour which have been devised under this usurpation and was a declaration of war against that authority which legislates laws not permitted by God. It was no secret to the Arabs — who knew their language very well and knew the real meaning of the message, **"La ilaha illa Allah"** — what its significance was in relation to their traditions, their rule and their power. Hence they greeted this call — this revolutionary message — with anger, and fought against it with that vigour which is known to everyone.

Why did this call begin in this manner? And why did the Divine wisdom decide that this call be confronted in its initial stages with trials?

* * *

At the time of the Prophet's call to Messengership, the land and the wealth of the Arabs was not in the hands of the Arabs but was in the hands of other people.

In the north, Syria was under the Romans, who appointed local Arab rulers. Similarly, in the south, Yemen was under the tutelage of the Persian Empire and was ruled by Arabs under its domination. Arabs were masters only of Hijaz, Tihama and Najd, which were waterless deserts with a few oases here and there.

It is also well — known that Muhammed — peace be on him — was called **'al-Amin as — Sadiq'** (The Trustworthy and Truthful') by his people. Fifteen years before his Messengership began, the leaders of the Quraish had made him their arbiter in the incident of the placing of the Black Stone and had been pleased with his decision. His lineage was from the Banu Hashim, which was the noblest branch of the Quraish. It can therefore be said that Muhammad — peace be on him — was capable of kindling among his compatriots the fire of Arab nationalism and would thus have united them. They would have responded gladly to this call, for they were weary of continual tribal warfare and blood feuds. He would then have been able to free the Arab lands from the domination of Roman and Persian imperialism and would have been able to establish a united Arab state.

It can be said that if the Prophet — peace be on him — had called people in this way, instead of bearing tortures for thirteen years due to the opposition of the people in authority in the peninsula, the whole of Arabia would have accepted it.

It can be said that if Arabia had thus been united under his leadership and the authority had once devolved into his hands, he could have used all this to make them accept the belief in the Oneness of God, for which purpose he was sent, and to bring people to submit to their Sustainerafter they had submitted to his own human authority.

But the All — Knowing and All — Wise God did not lead His Prophet —

peace be on him — on this course. He led him to declare openly that there is no deity but God, and to bear patiently, with his few Companions, whatever trials came to them.

Why this? Obviously it was not for the sake of subjecting His Prophet — peace be on him — and the Believers to oppression. Indeed, He knows that there is no other way. The way is not to free the earth from Roman and Persian tyranny in order to replace it with Arab tyranny. All tyranny is wicked! The earth belongs to God and should be purified for God, and it cannot be purified for Him unless the banner, "No deity except God", is unfurled across the earth. Man is servant to God alone, and he can remain so only if he unfurls the banner, "No deity except God, — **"La ilaha illa Allah"** — as an Arab with the knowledge of his language understood it: no sovereignty except God's, no law except from God, and no authority of one man over another, as the authority in all respects belong to God. The 'grouping' of men which Islam proclaims is based on this faith alone, the faith in which all peoples of any race or color — Arabs, Romans or Persians — are equal under the banner of God.

And this is the way.

At the time of the Prophet's call to Messengership, Arab society was devoid of proper distribution of wealth and devoid of justice. A small group monopolized all wealth and commerce, which increased through usury. The great majority of the people were poor and hungry. The wealthy were also regarded as noble and distinguished, and the common people were not only deprived of wealth but also of dignity and honor. It can be said that Muhammad — peace be on him — was capable of starting a social movement, declaring war against the class of nobles and the wealthy, taking away their wealth and distributing it among the poor.

It can be said that had the Prophet — peace be on him — started such a movement, Arab society would have been divided into two classes, the great majority supporting the new movement because they were sick of the tyranny of wealth, nobility and power and a small minority's possessing these things, instead of the Prophet's having to confront the society with the Message of the Oneness of God, which remained beyond the reach of all except a few noble souls.

It can be said that after the majority had joined his movement and had given him the leadership, and after he had gained control of the minority of the rich, Muhammad - peace be on him - could then have used his position and power to impose the belief in the Oneness of God, for which task God had appointed him as His Prophet. Thus, first making human beings bow before his authority, he could have made them bow before the True God.

But the All-Knowing, the All-Wise God did not lead him to this course.

God knew that this was not the way. He knew that true social justice can come to a society only after all affairs have been submitted to the laws of God and the society as a whole is willing to accept the just division of wealth prescribed by Him, and every individual of the society, whether he be a giver or a taker, firmly believes that this system has been legislated by God Almighty, by obeying which he will not only prosper in this world but will be rewarded in the next. The society should not be in such a condition that some are driven by greed while others are burning with envy, that all the affairs of the society are decided by the sword and the gun, fear and threats, that the hearts of the population are desolate and their spirits are broken, as is the case under systems which are based on any authority other than God's.

* * *

At the time of the Prophet's call to Messengership, the moral level of Arabia was extremely low from every point of view. Only a few primitive tribal customs prevailed. Oppression was the rule of the day, as the famous poet Zuhair Selma has described:

> ***"One who does not defend himself with weapons will perish, And one who does not oppress will be oppressed'. Another famous saying of the Days of Ignorance points to this:***
>
> ***"Help your brother, whether he is the oppressor or being oppressed".***

Drinking and gambling were traditions of the society and people were proud of these habits. All the poetry of the Days of Ignorance revolves around the theme of wine and gaming. Turfah Abed says:

> ***"If there had not been three things for a young man's enjoyment,***
>
> ***Then I would not have cared for anything except some food.***
>
> ***One of their is my excelling others in the drinking of wine which is so potent that if you add water to it, it bubbles.***
>
> ***Drinking and entertainment and spending***

***Have been my life, and still are.***

***At last the time has come when the whole tribe has abandoned me,***

***As if I were a camel with a terrible itch".***

Fornication was rampant in various forms and was considered something to be proud of, as is the case among all ***jahili*** societies, old or new. 'Aisha — may God be pleased with her — describes the condition of society of the Days of Ignorance in the following words:

"There were four kinds of marriages during ***Jahiliyyah***. One was as we have it today; that is, a man would ask a person for the hand of his daughter or his ward in marriage, would pay the marriage — gift, and would marry her. The second type was that a man would tell his wife, in between her menstrual periods, to call such and such man and become pregnant by him. He would stay away from her and would not touch her until the signs of pregnancy appeared. If he then wished, he would have intercourse with her. He adopted this method to obtain a son of high lineage. A third form of marriage was polyandry. A group of men, less than ten, would come to a woman and have sexual intercourse with her. If she became pregnant and then gave birth to a child, and a few nights passed after childbirth, she would call them. No one could refuse this call. When they would all gather, she would tell them, 'You know the result. I have given birth to a child.' Then she would point to one of them and would say, 'This is his child.' The child would then be named after that person and would be considered his, and he could not deny this. A fourth form of marriage was that many men would go to a woman, and she was willing to accept any. Actually, these were prostitutes and would place a flag in front of their doors as a sign. Anyone who wished would go to them. If such a woman became pregnant, after the delivery many people would gather by her and would call an expert in recognizing resemblances. To whomever he would ascribe the child's paternity, the child would be considered his and he could not refuse it."[7]

It can be said that Muhammad — peace be on him — was capable of starting a movement of moral reform for the establishment of moral standards, for the purification of the society, and for self — evaluation. As is the case with every reformer, he would have found some upright and straight people who were also unhappy about the moral degeneration of their society. These people would certainly have come to him to join his reformist movement.

---

7 Bukhari, in the Book of Marriage.

Thus, one can say that if the Prophet — peace be on him — had chosen this course, he would have easily gathered a sizeable group. Because of their moral purity and spiritual fortitude, this group of people, more than others, would have accepted the belief in the Oneness of God would have carried the responsibilities pertaining to it. Thus the Prophet's call, "There is no deity except God," would have been spared the vigourous opposition which it encountered.

But God Most High knew that this way is not the way. He knew that morality can only be built on faith, a faith which provides criteria, creates values, defines the authority from which these criteria and values are to be derived, and prescribes the reward of the one who accepts this authority and the punishment of those who deviate or oppose. Without this kind of belief or the concept of a higher authority, all values remain unstable, and similarly morals based on them remain unstable — without accounting, without authority, without reward!

When, after hard work, belief became firm and the authority to which this belief refers was acknowledged, when people recognized their Sustainer and worshipped Him alone, when they became independent not only of other human beings but also of their own desires, and when **"La ilaha illa Allah"** became imprinted on their hearts — then God, through this faith and through the Believers, provided everything which was needed. God's earth became free of 'Romans and Persians,' not so that the authority of 'Arabs' might prevail, but only so that God's authority might be established and that the earth might be cleared of all the rebels against Him, whether they were Roman, Persian or Arab.

The society was freed from all oppression, and the Islamic system was established in which justice was God's justice and in which weighing was by God's balance. The banner of social justice was raised in the name of One God, and the name of the banner was Islam. No other name was added to it, and **"La ilaha illa Allah"** was written on it.

Morals were elevated, hears and souls were purified, and with the exception of a very few cases, there was no occasion even to enforce the limits and punishments which God has prescribed; for now conscience was the law — enforcer, and the pleasure of God, the hope of Divine reward, and the fear of God's anger took the place of police and punishments.

Mankind was uplifted in its social order, in its morals, in all of its life, to a zenith of perfection which had never been attained before and which cannot be attained afterwards except through Islam.

All this was possible because those who established this religion in the form of a state, a system and laws and regulations had first established it in their hearts and lives in the form of faith, character, worship and human relationships. They had been promised only one thing for the establishment of this religion — not victory or power, not even that this religion would be established by their hands, not related to anything of this world: — one promise, that of the Garden. That was the only promise given to them for all their striving, for all the trials which they had endured, for their steadfastness in the face of the opposition of the forces of ***Jahiliyyah*** to that call, "There is no deity except God," which is abhorrent to those who are in power in any age and place.

When God tried them and they proved steadfast, relinquishing their own personal desires, and when God Most High knew that they were not waiting for any reward in this world, now were they desirous to see the victory of this message and the establishment of this Religion on earth by their hands, when their hearts became free of pride of lineage, of nationality, of country, of tribe, of household — in short, when God Most High saw them to be morally pure — then He granted them the great trust, the conscious assumption of being God's representative on earth. Since they were pure in faith, the requirement for which is that God's sovereignty alone extend over hearts and consciences in human relationships and morals, in lives and possessions, in modes and manners, God Most High knew that they would be true guardians of the political authority, which would be entrusted to them so that they would establish the Divine law and the Divine justice. He knew they would not use it to benefit their own selves or their families or tribe or nation, but would dedicate this authority purely to the service of God's religion and laws, as they knew that the true source of authority is God alone and that they were only trustees.

If the call of Islam had not started in this manner, discarding all banners other than "There is no deity except God," and if it had not taken that path which apparently was difficult and trying but which in reality was easy and blessed, then it would not have been possible to establish this blessed system with this high standard.

Had this call come in its initial stages as a national call or a social movement or a reformist attempt, or had it attached other labels to the call of "**La ilaha illa Allah**," then this blessed system would never have been for the sake of God alone.

* * *

The Meccan period of the Qur'an has this glorious attribute, that it imprints "There is no deity except God" on hearts and minds, and teaches

Muslims to adopt this method and no other — in spite of the fact that it appears difficult and to persist in this method.

The Qur'an concentrated all its teaching on the question of faith alone, not mentioning the details of the system which is to be based on it or the laws which are to regulate its affairs. The people who invite others to this Religion ought to ponder over this.

Indeed, it is the nature of this Religion which requires this particular method, as this Religion stands entirely on belief in the Oneness of God, and all its institution and laws are derived from this great principle. A simile for the Religion is a strong, tall tree whose shade spreads far and wide and whose branches reach toward the sky. Such a tree would naturally put its roots deep down into the earth and spread them over a wide area, in proportion to its size. The case of this Religion is similar. Its system extends into all aspects of life; it discusses all minor or major or affairs of mankind; it orders man's life — not only in this world but also in the world to come; it gives information about the Unseen as well as about the visible world; it not only deals with material things but also purifies intentions and ideas. It is thus like a tall, strong, wide spreading tree; clearly its roots must go down deep and be in proportion to its size.

This aspect of the nature of Islam define the way it is to be founded and organized: by implanting belief and strengthening it so that it seeps into the depths of the human soul. This is essential for its correct development, for only through this method can a relationship be secured between that part of the tree of religion which reaches upward and the roots which are in the depths of the earth.

When belief in "**La ilaha illa Allah**" penetrates into the deep recesses of the heart, it also penetrates through the whole system of life, which is a practical interpretation of this faith.

By this means, those who believe are already pleased with the system which this faith uniquely determines and submit in principle to all the laws and injunctions and details even before they are declared. Indeed, the spirit of submission is the first requirement of the faith. Through this spirit of submission the believers learn the Islamic regulations and laws with eagerness and pleasure. As soon as a command is given, the heads are bowed, and nothing more is required for its implementation except to hear it. In this manner, drinking was forbidden, usury was prohibited, and gambling was proscribed, and all the habits of the Days of Ignorance were abolished — abolished by a few verses of the Qur'an or by a few words from the lips of the Prophet — peace be on him. Compare this with the efforts of secular governments. At every stage they have to rely on legislation, administrative institutions, police and military power, propaganda and the press, and yet they can at most control what is done publicly, and society remains full of illegal and forbidden things.[8]

* * *

Another aspect of this religion ought to be considered. This is a practical religion; it has come to order the practical affairs of life. Thus it faces the question of practical conditions and determines whether to keep them, modify them or change them completely. Its legislation is therefore concerned only with those conditions which actually exist in that particular society which has already accepted the sovereignty of God. Islam is not a 'theory' based on 'assumptions;' rather it is a 'way of life' working with 'actuality,' Thus it is first necessary that a Muslim community come into existence which believes that "There is no deity except God," which commits itself to obey none but God, denying all other authority, and which challenges the legality of any law which is not based on this belief.

Only when such a society comes into being, faces various practical problems, and needs a system of law, then Islam initiates the constitution of law and injunctions, rules and regulations. It addresses only those people who in principle have already submitted themselves to its authority and have repudiated all other rules and regulations.

It is necessary that the believers in this faith be autonomous and have power in their own society, so that they may be able to implement this system and give currency to all its laws.

Moreover, power is also needed to legislate laws according to the needs of the group as these present themselves in its day — to — day affairs.

In Mecca the Muslims were not autonomous, nor did they have any influence in the society. Their practical life had not taken a permanent form so that they could have organized themselves according to the Divine Law (**al-Shari'ah**); hence no regulations and laws were revealed to them by God. They were taught only belief and those moral principles which follow from this belief after it penetrates the mind. Later, when an autonomous state came into existence in Medina, general laws were revealed and that system came into existence which satisfies the needs of a

---

8. Refer to **Fi Thilal al-Qur'an (In the Shade of the Qur'an)**, Vol. 5, pp. 78 — 85, to see how God forbade the drinking of alcohol. Then refer to Sayed Abul Hasan Ali Nadvi's book, **The Loss to the World Due to the Decline of Muslims**, quoting Abul 'Ala Maududi's **Tanqihat** to see how the United States failed in its efforts to prohibit alcohol.

Muslim community, and the power of the state was behind its enforcement.

God Most High did not desire that all laws and regulations be revealed during the Meccan period so that Muslims would have a ready — made system to be applied as soon as they reached Medina; this is out of character for this religion. Islam is more practical than this and has more foresight; it does not find solution to hypothetical problems. It first looks at the prevailing conditions, and if it finds a viable society which, according to its form, conditions or temperament, is a Muslim society, which has submitted itself to the law of God and is weary of laws emanating from other sources, then indeed this religion provides a method for the legislation of laws according to the needs of such a society.

People who demand from Islam that it provide theories, and that it provide a completed constitution for its system, and that it provide laws, while they observe that there is not a single society on earth which has rejected man — made systems and agreed to enforce the **Shari'ah**, in addition to having political power for such enforcement, show that they are ignorant of the character of this religion and the way it operates in life. They are also ignorant of the purpose for which God revealed His religion.

What these people want is that Islam change its character, its method and its history and be reduced to the level of ordinary human theories and laws. They want a short — cut solution to satisfy their immediate desires, which are simply a product of the defeatist mentality in their spirits in the face of valueless, man — made laws. They want Islam to become a mere collection of abstractions and theories, the subject of whose application is non — existent conditions. But the course prescribed by God for this religion is the same as it was earlier. First, belief ought to be imprinted on hearts and rule over consciences — that belief which demands that people should not bow before anyone except God or derive laws from any other source. Then, when such a group of people is ready and also gains practical control of society, various laws will be legislated according to the practical needs of that society.

This is what God has intended for this religion. It cannot be other than what God intends, no matter what people desire.

The callers to Islam should understand that when they invite people toward the revival of religion, they should invite them to accept Islam's fundamental belief — even though these people call themselves Muslims or their birth certificates register them as Muslims. The people ought to know that Islam means to accept the creed **"La ilaha illa Allah"** in its deepest sense, which is this: that every aspect of life should be under the sovereignty of God, and those who rebel against God's sovereignty and usurp it for themselves should be opposed; that this belief should be accepted by their hearts and minds and should be applied in their ways of living and in their practices.

When the revival of this religion starts among a people, this aspect of it must have first priority. The first Islamic call was based on it; thirteen complete years of the Meccan period of the Qur'an were devoted to this Message. When a group of people enters this religion in the true sense, only then can it be considered a 'Muslim group.' Only such a group has the capability of giving a concrete form to the Islamic system in its social life, because such a group has agreed to base its entire life on Islam and to obey God in all aspects of life. Thus, when such a society actually comes into being and the basic teachings of Islam are its guide, it will proceed to formulate laws and regulations for the existing practical needs according to the general teachings of Islam. This is the correct order for bringing about a practical, realistic and wise Islamic system.

Some sincere people who do not understand the real character of our religion are in a hurry. They have not understood that this is the way prescribed by the All — Knowing and All — Wise God. They say that if people are taught Islam's fundamentals and the Islamic laws, then the way for inviting them to Islam will become easy and people will automatically become sympathetic to Islam.

This is their wishful thinking, due to their impatience. This is akin to the idea which could have been presented to the Prophet himself — peace be on him — and which we have described in earlier pages; that is, that if the Prophet — peace be on him — had started his call with nationalism, or economic revolution, or reformist movement, his way would have become easier

It is essential that hearts be exclusively devoted to God alone, accepting His law with full submission and rejecting all other laws — from the very beginning, even before the details are shown to attract them.

The love of the Divine Law **al-Shari'ah** should be a consequence of pure submission to God and of freedom from servitude to anyone else, and not because it Is superior to other systems in such and such details.

No doubt the **Shari'ah** is best since it comes from God; the laws of His creatures can hardly be compared to the laws given by the Creator. But this point is not the basis of the Islamic call. The basis of the message is that one should accept the **Shari'ah** without any question and reject allother laws in any shape or form. This is Islam. There is no other meaning of

Islam. One who if attracted to this basic Islam has already resolved this problem; he will not require any persuasion through showing its beauty and superiority. This is one of the realities of the faith.

* * *

Next, we ought to discuss how the Qur'an solved the problem of belief and faith during the thirteen years of Meccan life. The Qur'an did not present this in the form of a theory or a theology, nor did it present it in the style which is common to our scholastic writings on the subject of the Oneness of God.

None of this; The Qur'an always appeals to human nature and draws our attention to the signs of God which are within man's soul itself and are all around him. It liberates human nature from superstitions, polishes man's native intelligence to the utmost degree, and opens up windows to the world and makes man appreciate the intricate processes of God's nature.

This is a general aspect. A particular aspect is that the Qur'an, on the basis of this belief, started a struggle in actual life against false ideas and traditions under which human nature had become helpless. To confront these special circumstances, it would not have been desirable to present Islam in the form of a theory. It took the form of a direct confrontation, with a determination to rend the curtains which had fallen on the hearts and minds of people and to break into pieces all those walls which were standing between man and the truth. Similarly, intellectual argumentation, based on verbal logic, which was the hallmark of the scholastic theology of later times, was not a proper style for it. The Qur'an was struggling against the entire human environment as it existed. It was addressing itself to the whole of humanity which was drowned under the vast ocean of corruption. The style of theology would have been useless for it because, although Islamic belief is a belief, its main program is in the practical sphere of life; it does not remain circumscribed in theoretical discussions and the speculations of theology.

The Qur'an on the one hand constructs faith in the hearts of the Muslim community and on the other attacks the surrounding ***Jahiliyyah*** through this community, while struggling to remove all the ***jahili*** influences which are found in the ideas, practices and morals of the Muslim community. The construction of Islamic belief occurred under these stormy conditions, and not in the form of a theology or theory or scholastic argument. It was rather as an active, organic and vital movement, the concrete representation of which was the Muslim community. The growth of the Muslim community, including its ideas, morals, education and training, was due to its belief.

The evolution of this movement was wholly the practical manifestation of the evolution of its beliefs, and this is the true method of Islam which reflects its nature and its spirit.

The bearers of the Islamic message should keep in mind this dynamic method of Islam which we have described above. They ought to know that the stage of the construction of belief, which spread over the long period of Meccan life in this fashion, was not separate from the stage of practical organization, under which an Islamic community came into existence. It was not a stage of teaching and learning 'the theory'! It was a single stage in which, at the same time, the seed of faith was implanted and a community was organized, giving a practical structure to the Islamic teachings. Hence in the future, whenever there are attempts at the revival of Islam, this comprehensive method should be adopted.

Thus the stage of constructing the faith should be long, and it should be gradual. Every step should be taken with firmness. This stage should not be spent in teaching the theory of beliefs but in translating the belief into a living reality. First it should be implanted in the hearts of men; it should materialize in a dynamic social system whose internal and external growth reflects the evolution of the belief. It ought to be a dynamic movement which challenges ***Jahiliyyah*** both in theory and in practice, so that it becomes a living faith which grows while struggling against the surrounding forces.

It is an error and what an error! — to think that Islam can evolve in the form of an abstract theory limited to intellectual learning and cultural knowledge. Beware of this danger, beware!

The Qur'an did not come down at once but took thirteen years to construct and strengthen the structure of faith. Had God wanted, He would have revealed the entire Qur'an at once and then left the Companions to learn it for a period of approximately thirteen years so that the Believers would master the 'Islamic theory;

But God Most High did not choose this method; He wanted something else. He wanted to lay the foundations of a community, a movement and a belief simultaneously. He wanted the community and the movement to be founded on belief, while with the dynamic progress of the community the faith also grew. He wanted faith to grow with the progress of the community, while the practical life of the community was at the same time a mirror of the faith. God Most High knew that men and societies are not founded overnight, but that it takes as much time to construct and develop a faith as it takes to organize a community, so that as the faith is completed, simultaneously a strong community also comes into existence which is the true representation and practical interpretation of the faith.

* * *

This is the character of our religion, and the Meccan period of the Qur'an testifies to it. We should be aware of this character and should not try to change it by being impatient or falling under the influence of a defeatist mentality in the presence of valueless, man — made theories. Through this particular quality of Islam, the first Muslim community came into existence, and in the future, whenever a Muslim community is to be created in the world, it can be created only by this method and in relation to this character.

We should be aware that any attempt to change the living faith of Islam, which is intended to penetrate into the veins and arteries of a vital society and to be a concrete organized movement, into purely theoretical teachings and academic discussions, is an attempt to show the superiority of the 'Islamic theory' over the valueless and useless theories formulated by man, and is not only erroneous but also dangerous.

The requirement of Islamic belief is that it take shape in living souls, in an active organization, and in a viable community. It should take the form of a movement struggling against the ***jahili*** environment while also trying to remove the influences of ***jahili*** society in its followers, because they were people of ***Jahiliyyah*** before the faith entered their souls, and the influence of ***Jahiliyyah*** might have remained in their hearts and minds as well as in their lives. Islamic belief has a much wider range of action than simply academic discussions, as it not only addresses itself to hearts and minds but also includes practices and morals.

The Divine attributes, the universe, life, man, are all included in the Islamic concept, which is not only very comprehensive and perfect but also realistic and constructive. Islam, because of its very nature, abhors being reduced to pure thought — this being against its nature and also against its ultimate aim — and loves to appear personified in human beings, in a living organization and in a practical movement. Its method is to grow through the agency of living persons and through a dynamic movement and an active organization in such a way that its theory comes to fruition at the same time as its practical applications. It never remains an abstract theory but develops side — by — side with practice.

As for the idea that we should first perfect Islam as a theory, bringing it about later in the world of action, this is an error and is dangerous, being against the nature of Islam, its purpose and its structural elements. God

Most High Says:

وَقُرْاٰنًا فَرَقْنٰهُ لِتَقْرَاَهٗ عَلَى النَّاسِ عَلٰى مُكْثٍ وَّ نَزَّلْنٰهُ تَنْزِيْلًا ﴿١٠٦﴾

***"We have revealed this Qur'an little by little so that you may recite it to people at intervals, and We have revealed it gradually" (17:106)***

Gradualness and teaching at intervals is desired, so that a 'living community' based on its beliefs may come into existence, and not merely a 'theory.'

The message — bearers of Islam should fully understand that this is a Divine religion and that its method, which is harmonious with its nature, is also based on Divine guidance. It is not possible to establish this religion without following its particular method.

One should also understand that this religion has come to change not only the beliefs and practices of people but also the method of bringing about these changes in beliefs and practices. This religion constructs beliefs together with forming a community; it also develops its system of thought while it spends its energy in enforcing its practical aspects. Thus the establishment of its particular system of thought, its particular beliefs and its particular way of living does not require different methods but is fulfilled simultaneously.

From the above explanation we know that this religion has a particular method of action. Now we ought to know that this method is eternal. It is not related to any particular stage or to any special conditions and environment peculiar to the first Muslim community. Indeed, this religion cannot be established — at any time — except through this method.

Islam's function is to change people's beliefs and actions as well as their outlook and way of thinking. Its method is Divinely — ordained and is entirely different from all the valueless methods of short — sighted human beings.

We cannot receive the Divine guidance or live according to it unless we adopt the Divinely — ordained method, the method which God intended for reforming human thought and practice.

* * *

When we try to make Islam into a 'theory' to be studied, we remove the Divine method and Divine outlook from its character, and we reduce it to the level of a man — made system of thought, as if the Divine method were inferior to man's methods, and as if we wanted to elevate the system of thought and action ordained by God to the level of the systems of His creatures!

This point of view is extremely dangerous, and this defeatism is ruinous.

The function of this Divine system which is given to us — we, who are the callers to Islam — is to provide a certain style of thinking, purified from all those ***jahili*** styles and ways of thinking which are current in the world and which have poisoned our culture by depriving us of our own mind. If we try to change this religion in a way which is alien to its nature and which is borrowed from the ways of the predominant ***Jahiliyyah***, we will deprive it of the function it has come to perform for humanity. We will deprive ourselves of the opportunity of getting rid of the yoke of the ***jahili*** ways current in our time, which dominate our minds.

This aspect of the situation is full of danger, and the resulting loss will be disastrous.

The ways of thought and action for the founding of the Islamic system are not less important or less necessary than this Islamic belief and way of life, nor are they separate from each other. Although it may seem very attractive to us to keep expounding on the beauties of the Islamic beliefs and system, we should not forget this fact: that Islam can never become a practical way of life or a dynamic movement through these means. We should also realize that this way of presenting Islam does not benefit anyone except those who are working for the Islamic movement, and even this group can benefit from it only to such an extent as corresponds with its stage of development.

I therefore repeat that Islamic belief should at once materialize into a practical movement, and from the very instant this comes into being, the movement should become a real representation and an accurate mirror of its belief.

I will also repeat that this is the method which is natural to the Divinely revealed religion of Islam, and that this method is the most superior and lasting and is extremely effective.

It is closer to human nature that all those methods which present Islam to people in the form of a complete and fixed theory, before these people have engaged in a practical movement and before this has become a living reality in their hearts, growing step by step in translating this theory into actuality.

* * *

If this is the correct method for the fundamentals of Islamic belief, it is even more correct with respect to the particulars of the organizational structure and its legal details.

The ***Jahiliyyah*** which has surrounded us, and which weighs heavily on the minds of some sincere workers for Islam who become impatient and want to see all the stages of the Islamic system come into existence very rapidly, has raised a very delicate question indeed. It asks them: What are the details of the system to which you are calling? How much research have you done? How many articles have you prepared and how many subjects have you written about? Have you constituted its jurisprudence on new principles? — as if nothing were lacking for the enforcement of the Islamic Law except research in jurisprudence (Fiqh) and its details, as if everyone had agreed upon the sovereignty of God and were willing to submit to His laws, as if the only factor remaining were the non — existence of ***Mujtahidin***[9] who would supply a modernised version of Islamic jurisprudence. This is a vulgar joke on Islam, and every person who has any respect for this religion should raise himself above it.

By these tactics, ***Jahiliyyah*** wants to find an excuse to reject the Divine system and to perpetuate the slavery of one man over another. It desires to turn away the power of Muslims from the work of establishing the Divinely — ordained way of life in order that they may not go beyond the stage of belief to the stage of a dynamic movement. It wants to distort the very nature of this method — the method in which Islamic belief matures through the struggle of its movement, in which the details of the Islamic system develop through practical striving, and in which laws are disseminated to solve practical problems and actual difficulties.

It is the duty of Muslims to expose these tactics and reduce them to dust, to reject this ridiculous proposal of the 'reconstruction of Islamic law' for a society which is neither willing to submit to the law of God nor expresses any weariness with laws emanating from sources other than God. Such talk is a way of diverting attention from real and earnest work, and is a method through which the workers for Islam can be made to waste their time in building castles in the air. Thus it is their duty to expose these treacherous tactics.

It is their duty to adopt the method of the Islamic movement which is harmonious with this religion. This method is the source of power for this religion, as well as a source of power for them.

Islam and the method of revival of Islam are both equally important;

---

9 Those Muslims whose knowledge of Islamic sources of law is so deep that they can with validity exercise independent judgment in matters pertaining to legal details.

there is no difference between them. Any other method, however attractive it may be, cannot bring about the establishment of Islam. Other methods can work for the establishment of — man — made systems, but are incapable of establishing our system. Thus it is as necessary to follow this particular method for the establishment of Islam as it is to obey the way of life it outlines and to believe in its articles of faith.

إِنَّ هَٰذَا الْقُرْآنَ يَهْدِي لِلَّتِي هِيَ أَقْوَمُ

***"Indeed, this Qur'an leads to a way which is straight."*** *(17:9)*

## *CHAPTER 3*

# THE CHARACTERISTICS OF THE ISLAMIC SOCIETY AND THE CORRECT METHOD FOR ITS FORMATION

The message of Islam brought by the Messenger of God, Muhammad — peace be on him — was the last link in the long chain of invitations toward God by the noble Prophets. Throughout history, this message has remained the same: that human beings should recognise that their true Sustainer and Lord is One God, that they should submit to Him Alone, and that the lordship of man be eliminated. Except for a few people here and there in history, mankind as a whole has never denied the existence of God and His sovereignty over the universe; it has rather erred in comprehending the real attributes of God, or in taking other gods besides God as His associates. This association with God has been either in belief and worship, or in accepting the sovereignty of others besides God. Both of these aspects are **Shirk**[10] in the sense that they take human beings away from the religion of God, which was brought by the Prophets. After each Prophet, there was a period during which people understood this religion, but then gradually later generations forgot it and returned to ***Jahiliyyah***. They started again on the way of **Shirk**, sometimes in their belief and worship and sometimes in their submission to the authority of others, and sometimes in both.

Throughout every period of human history the call toward God has had one nature. Its purpose is '**Islam**', which means to bring human beings into submission to God, to free them from servitude to other human beings so that they may devote themselves to the One True God, to deliver them

10 **Shirk** is an Arabic word which refers to ascribing the attributes, power or authority of God to others besides Him and/or worshipping others besides Him.

from the clutches of human lordship and man — made laws, value systems and traditions so that they will acknowledge the sovereignty and authority of the One True God and follow His law in all spheres of life. The Islam of Muhammad — peace be on him — came for this purpose, as well as the messages of the earlier Prophets. The entire universe is under the authority of God, and man, being a small part of it, necessarily obeys the physical laws governing the universe. It is also necessary that the same authority be acknowledged as the law — giver for human life. Man should not cut himself off from this authority to develop a separate system and a separate scheme of life. The growth of a human being, his conditions of health and disease, and his life and death are under the scheme of those natural laws which come from God; even in the consequences of his voluntary actions he is helpless before the universal laws. Man cannot change the practice of God in the laws prevailing in the universe. It is therefore desirable that he should also follow Islam in those aspects of his life in which he is given a choice and should make the Divine Law the arbiter in all matters of life so that there may be harmony between man and the rest of the universe.[11]

***Jahiliyyah***, on the other hand, is one man's lordship over another, and in this respect it is against the system of the universe and brings the involuntary aspect of human life into conflict with its voluntary aspect. This was that ***Jahiliyyah*** which confronted every Prophet of God, including the last Prophet — peace be on him — in their call toward submission to One God. This ***Jahiliyyah*** is not an abstract theory; in fact, under certain circumstances it has no theory at all. It always takes the form of a living movement in a society which has its own leadership, its own concepts and values, and its own traditions, habits and feelings. It is an organized society and there is a close cooperation and loyalty between its individuals, and it is always ready and alive to defend its existence consciously or unconsciously. It crushes all elements which seem to be dangerous to its personality.

When ***Jahiliyyah*** takes the form, not of a 'theory' but of an active movement in this fashion, then any attempt to abolish this ***Jahiliyyah*** and to bring people back to God which presents Islam merely as a theory will be undesirable, rather useless. ***Jahiliyyah*** controls the practical world, and for its support there is a living and active organization. In this situation, mere theoretical efforts to fight it cannot even be equal, much less superior, to it. When the purpose is to abolish the existing system and to replace it with a new system which in its character, principles and all its general and

11 See Towards Understanding Islam, by A. A. Maududi, for an explanation of this point.

particular aspects, is different from the controlling *jahili* system, then it stands to reason that this new system should also come into the battlefield as an organized movement and a viable group. It should come into the battlefield with a determination that its strategy, its social organization, and the relationship between its individuals should be firmer and more powerful than the existing *jahili* system.

The theoretical foundation of Islam, in every period of history, has been to witness **"La ilaha illa Allah"** — "There" is no deity except God" — which means to bear witness that the only true deity is God, that He is the Sustainer, that He is the Ruler of the universe, and that He is the Real Sovereign; to believe in Him in one's heart, to worship Him Alone, and to put into practice His laws. Without this complete acceptance of "**La ilaha illa Allah**", which differentiates the one who says he is a Muslim from a non — Muslim, there cannot be any practical significance to this utterance, nor will it have any weight according to Islamic law.

Theoretically, to establish it means that people should devote their entire lives in submission to God, should not decide any affair on their own, but must refer to God's injunctions concerning it and follow them. We know of God's guidance through only one source, that is, through the Messenger of God — peace be on him. Thus, in the second part of the Islamic creed, we bear witness '**Wa ashhaduanna Muhammadar Rasul Allah**" — "And I bear witness that Muhammad is the Messenger of God".

It is therefore necessary that Islam's theoretical foundation — belief — materialize in the form of an organized and active group from the very beginning. It is necessary that this group separate itself from the *jahili* society, becoming independent and distinct from the active and organized *jahili* society whose aim is to block Islam. The centre of this new group should be a new leadership, the leadership which first came in the person of the Prophet — peace be on him — himself, and after him was delegated to those who strove for bringing people back to God's sovereignty, His authority and His laws. A person who bears witness that there is no deity except God and that Muhammad is God's Messenger should cut off his relationship of loyalty from the *jahili* society, which he has forsaken, and from *jahili* leadership, whether it be in the guise of priests, magicians or astrologers, or in the form of political, social or economic leadership, as was the case of the Quraish in the time of the Prophet — peace be on him. He will have to give his complete loyalty to the new Islamic movement and to the Muslim leadership.

This decisive step must be taken at the very moment a person says, "**La**

**ilaha illa Allah, Muhammadar Rasul Allah**" with his tongue. The Muslim society cannot come into existence without this. It cannot come into existence simply as a creed in the hearts of individual Muslims, however numerous they may be, unless they become an active, harmonious and cooperative group, distinct by itself, whose different elements, like the limbs of a human body, work together for its formation, its strengthening, its expansion, and for its defence against all those elements which attack its system, working under a leadership which is independent of the ***jahili*** leadership, which organizes its various efforts into one harmonious purpose, and which prepares for the strengthening and widening of their Islamic character and directs them to abolish the influences of their opponent, the ***jahili*** life.

Islam was founded in this manner. It was founded on a creed which, although concise, included the whole of life. This creed immediately brought into action a viable and dynamic group of people who became independent and separate from the ***jahili*** society, immediately challenging it; it never came as an abstract theory devoid of practical existence. And, in the future it can be brought about only in this manner. There is no other way for the revival of Islam in the shade of ***Jahiliyyah***, in whatever age or country it appears, except to follow its natural character and to develop it into a movement and an organic system.

* * *

When Islam, according to the method described above, starts a Muslim community on this basis, forms it into an active group, and makes this faith the sole basis for the relationship between the individuals of this group, its ultimate aim is to awaken the 'humanity of man', to develop it, to make it powerful and strong, and to make it the most dominant factor among all the aspects found in man's being. It seeks to implement this purpose through its teachings, its rules, its laws and injunctions.

Some human characteristics are common with those of animals, even with those of inorganic matter. This has misled the exponents of 'scientific ***Jahiliyyah***' to consider man to be nothing more than an animal, or even than inorganic matter! But in spite of the characteristics which man shares with animals and inorganic matter, man possesses certain other characteristics which distinguish him and make him a unique creation. Even the exponents of 'scientific ignorance' were forced to admit this, the evidence of observational facts choking them; but even then, their admission of this fact is neither sincere nor unequivocal.[12]

---

12 Foremost among the modern Darwinists is Julian Huxley.

In this respect the service rendered by Islam's pure way of life has produced concrete and valuable results. Islam based the Islamic society on the association of belief alone, instead of the low associations based on race and colour, language and country, regional and national interests. Instead of stressing those traits which are common to both man and animal, it promoted man's human qualities, nurtured them and made them the dominant factor. Among the concrete and brilliant results of this attitude was that the Islamic society became an open and all — inclusive community in which people of various races, nations, languages and colours were members, there remaining no trace of these low animalistic traits. The rivers of higher talents and various abilities of all races of mankind flowed into this vast ocean and mixed in it. Their intermingling gave rise to a high level of civilization in a very short span of time, dazzling the whole world, and compounding the essences of all the human capabilities, ideas and wisdom of that period, in spite of the fact in those times travel was difficult and the means of communication were slow.

In this great Islamic society Arabs, Persians, Syrians, Egyptians, Moroccans, Turks, Chinese, Indians, Romans, Greeks, Indonesians, Africans were gathered together — in short, peoples of all nations and all races. Their various characteristics were united, and with mutual cooperation, harmony and unity they took part in the construction of the Islamic community and Islamic culture. This marvellous civilization was not an 'Arabic civilization', even for a single day; it was purely an 'Islamic civilization'. It was never a 'nationality' but always a 'community of belief'.

Thus they all came together on an equal footing in the relationship of love, with their minds set upon a single goal; thus they used their best abilities, developed the qualities of their race to the fullest, and brought the essence of their personal, national and historical experiences for the development of this one community, to which they all belonged on an equal footing and in which their common bond was through their relationship to their Sustainer. In this community their 'humanity' developed without any hindrance. These are characteristics which were never achieved by any other group of people in the entire history of mankind!

The most distinguished and best known society in ancient history is considered to be the Roman Empire. Peoples of various races, languages and temperaments came together in this society, but all this was not based on 'human relationship' nor was any sublime faith the uniting factor among them; rather their society was ordered on a class system, the class of 'nobles' and the class of 'slaves', throughout the Empire. Moreover, the Roman race — in general-had the leadership and the other races were considered its subjects. Hence this society could not achieve that height which was achieved by the Islamic society and did not bring those blessings which were brought by the Islamic society.

Various societies have also appeared in modern times. For example, consider the British Empire. It is like the Roman society to which it is an heir. It is based on national greed, in which the British nation has the leadership and exploits those colonies annexed by the Empire. The same is true of other European empires. The Spanish and Portuguese Empires in their times, and the French Empire, all are equal in respect to oppression and exploitation. Communism also wanted to establish a new type of society, demolishing the walls of race and color, nation and geographical region, but it is not based on 'human relationship' but on a 'class system'. Thus the communist society is like the Roman society with a reversal of emphasis; there nobles had distinction, while here the proletariat has distinction. The underlying emotion of this class is hatred and envy of other classes. Such a selfish and vengeful society cannot but excite base emotions in its individuals. The very basis of it is laid down in exciting animalistic characteristics, and in developing and strengthening them. Thus, in its view, the most fundamental needs of a human being are those which are common with the animals, that is, 'food, shelter and sex. From its point of view, the whole of human history is nothing but a struggle for food!

Islam, then, is the only Divine way of life which brings out the noblest human characteristics, developing and using them for the construction of human society. Islam has remained unique in this respect to this day. Those who deviate from this system and want some other system, whether it be based on nationalism, colour and race, class struggle, or similar corrupt theories, are truly enemies of mankind! They do not want man to develop those noble characteristics which have been given to him by his Creator nor do they wish to see a human society benefit from the harmonious blending of all those capabilities, experiences and characteristics which have been developed among the various races of mankind.

God Most High says about such people:

قُلْ هَلْ نُنَبِّئُكُمْ بِالْأَخْسَرِينَ أَعْمَالًا ﴿١٠٣﴾ الَّذِينَ ضَلَّ سَعْيُهُمْ فِي الْحَيٰوةِ
الدُّنْيَا وَهُمْ يَحْسَبُونَ أَنَّهُمْ يُحْسِنُونَ صُنْعًا ﴿١٠٤﴾ أُولٰٓئِكَ الَّذِينَ كَفَرُوا بِاٰيٰتِ
رَبِّهِمْ وَلِقَآئِهٖ فَحَبِطَتْ أَعْمَالُهُمْ فَلَا نُقِيمُ لَهُمْ يَوْمَ الْقِيٰمَةِ وَزْنًا ﴿١٠٥﴾ ذٰلِكَ
جَزَآؤُهُمْ جَهَنَّمُ بِمَا كَفَرُوا وَاتَّخَذُوٓا اٰيٰتِي وَرُسُلِي هُزُوًا ﴿١٠٦﴾

> *"Say: Shall We tell you who will be the greatest losers in their deeds? Those whose effort goes astray in the present life, while they think that they are doing good deeds. Those are they who disbelieve in the signs of their Lord and in the encounter with Him. Their works have failed, and on the Day of Resurrection We shall not assign to them any value. That is their payment — Hell — for that they were unbelievers and took My signs and My Messengers in mockery."*
>
> *(18:103-106)*

God Almighty speaks the truth.

## *CHAPTER 4*

# JIHAAD[13] IN THE CAUSE OF GOD

The great scholar Ibn Qayyim, in his book Zad al-Mi'ad, has a chapter entitled "The Prophet's Treatment of the Unbelievers and the Hypocrites from the Beginning of His Messengership Until His Death." In this chapter, this scholar has summed up the nature of Islamic **Jihaad**.

"The first revelation from God which came to the Prophet — peace be on him — was **'Iqraa, bisme Rabbika alladhee** ...'('Read, in the name of Your Sustainer, Who created ...'). This was the beginning of the Prophethood. God commanded the Prophet — peace be on him — to recite this in his heart. The commandment to preach had not yet come. Then God revealed **'Ya ayyuha al-Muddathir, qumfandhir'** (O you who are enwrapped in your mantle, arise and warn'). Thus, the revelation of 'Iqraa' was his appointment to Prophet — hood, while **'Ya ayyuha al-muddathir'** was his appointment to Messengership. Later God commanded the Prophet — peace be on him — to warn his near relatives, then his people, then the Arabs who were around them, then all of Arabia, and finally the whole world. Thus for thirteen years after the beginning of his Messengership, he called people to God through preaching, without fighting or **Jizyah**,[14] and was commanded to restrain himself and to practice patience and forbearance. Then he was commanded to migrate, and later permission was given to fight. Then he was commanded to fight those who fought him, and to restrain himself from those who did not make war with him. Later he was commanded to fight the polytheists until God's religion was fully established. After the command for **Jihaad** came, the non —

---

13 Literally, 'striving'. This Arabic word denotes any form of activity, either personal or community — wide, of Muslims in attempting to strive for the cause of God and for the sake of Islam.

14 A tax levied by Muslims on non — Muslim men in areas governed by Muslims, in lieu of military service.

believers were divided into three categories: one, those with whom there was peace; two, the people with whom the Muslims were at war; and three, the **Dhimmies.**[15] It was commanded that as long as the non — believers with whom he had a peace treaty met their obligations, he should fulfill the articles of the treaty, but if they broke this treaty, then they should be given notice of having broken it; until then, no war should be declared. If they persisted, then he should fight with them. When the chapter entitled 'Bra't' was revealed, the details of treatment of these three kinds of non — believers were described. It was also explained that war should be declared against those from among the 'People of the Book'[16] who declare open enmity, until they agree to pay Jizyah or accept Islam. Concerning the polytheists and the hypocrites, it was commanded in this chapter that **Jihaad** be declared against them and that they be treated harshly. The Prophet — peace be on him — carried on **Jihaad** against the polytheists by fighting and against the hypocrites by preaching and argument. In the same chapter, it was commanded that the treaties with the polytheists be brought to an end at the period of their expiration. In this respect, the people with whom there were treaties were divided into three categories: The first, those who broke the treaty and did not fulfill its terms. He was ordered to fight against them: he fought with them and was victorious. The second were those with whom the treaty was made for a stated term; they had not broken this treaty nor helped anyone against the Prophet — peace be on him — Concerning them, God ordered that these treaties be completed to their full term. The third kind were those with whom there was neither a treaty nor were they fighting against the Prophet — peace be on him or those with whom no term of expiration was stated. Concerning these, it was commanded that they be given four months' notice it expiration, at the end of which they should be considered open enemies and fought with. Thus, those who broke the treaty were fought against, and those who did not have any treaty or had an indeterminate period of expiration were given four months' period of grace, and terms were kept with those with whom the treaty was due to expire. All the latter people embraced Islam even before the term expired, and the non — Muslims of the state paid Jizyah. Thus, after the revelation of the chapter 'Bra't', the unbelievers were of three kinds: adversaries in war, people with treaties, and **Dhimmies**. The people with treaties eventually became Muslims, so there were only two

15 Literally meaning 'responsibility', **Dhimmies** refers to the non — Muslim peoples residing in a Muslim state for whose protection and rights the Muslim government was responsible.

16 Christians and Jews.

kinds left: people at war and **Dhimmies**. The people at war were always afraid of him. Now the people of the whole world were of three kinds: One, the Muslims who believed in him; two, those with whom he had peace; and three, the opponents who kept fighting him. As far as the hypocrites were concerned, God commanded the Prophet — peace be on him — to accept their appearances and leave their intentions to God, and carry on **Jihaad** against them by argument and persuasion. He was commanded not to pray at their funerals nor to pray at their graves, nor should he ask forgiveness from God for them, as their affair was with God. So this was the practice of the Prophet — peace be on him — concerning his enemies among the non — believers and the hypocrites."

In this description we find a summary of the stages of Islamic **Jihaad** presented in an excellent manner. In this summary we find all the distinctive and far — reaching characteristics of the dynamic movement of the true religion; we should ponder over them for deep study. Here, however, we will confine ourselves to a few explanatory remarks.

First, the method of this religion is very practical. This movement treats people as they actually are and uses resources which are in accordance with practical conditions. Since this movement comes into conflict with the ***Jahiliyyah*** which prevails over ideas and beliefs, and which has a practical system of life and a political and material authority behind it, the Islamic movement had to produce parallel resources to confront this ***Jahiliyyah***. This movement uses the methods of preaching and persuasion for reforming ideas and beliefs; and it uses physical power and **Jihaad** for abolishing the organizations and authorities of the ***Jahili*** system which prevents people from reforming their ideas and beliefs but forces them to obey their erroneous ways and make them serve human lords instead of the Almighty Lord. This movement does not confine itself to mere preaching to confront physical power, as it also does not use compulsion for changing the ideas of people. These two principles are equally important in the method of this religion. Its purpose is to free those people who wish to be freed from enslavement to men so that they may serve God alone.

The second aspect of this religion is that it is a practical movement which progresses stage by stage, and at every stage it provides resources according to the practical needs of the situation and prepares the ground for the next one. It does not face practical problems with abstract theories, nor does it confront various stages with unchangeable means. Those who talk about **Jihaad** in Islam and quote Qur'anic verses do not take into account this aspect, nor do they understand the nature of the various stages through which this movement develops, or the relationship of the verses revealed at various occasions with each stage. Thus, when they speak about **Jihaad**, they speak clumsily and mix up the various stages, distorting the whole concept of**Jihaad** and deriving from the Qur'anic verses final principles and generalities for which there is no justification. This is because they regard every verse of the Qur'an as if it were the final principle of this religion. This group of thinkers, who are a product of the sorry state of the present Muslim generation, have nothing but the label of Islam and have laid down their spiritual and rational arms in defeat. They say, "Islam has prescribed only defensive war"! and think that they have done some good for their religion by depriving it of its method, which is to abolish all injustice from the earth, to bring people to the worship of God alone, and to bring them out of servitude to others into the servants of the Lord. Islam does not force people to accept its belief, but it wants to provide a free environment in which they will have the choice of beliefs. What it wants is to abolish those oppressive political systems under which people are prevented from expressing their freedom to choose whatever beliefs they want, and after that it gives them complete freedom to decide whether they will accept Islam or not.

A third aspect of this religion is that the new resources or methods which it uses during its progressive movement do not take it away from its fundamental principles and aims. From the very first day, whether the Prophet — peace be on him — addressed his near relatives, or the Quraish, or the Arabs, or the entire world, his call was one and the same. He called them to the submission to One God and rejection of the lordship of other men. On this principle there is no compromise nor any flexibility. To attain this purpose, it proceeds according to a plan, which has a few stages, and every stage has its new resources, as we have described earlier.

A fourth aspect is that Islam provides a legal basis for the relationship of the Muslim community with other groups, as is clear from the quotation from Zad al-Mi'ad. This legal formulation is based on the principle that Islam — that is, submission to God — is a universal Message which the whole of mankind should accept or make peace with. No political system or material power should put hindrances in the way of preaching Islam. It should leave every individual free to accept or reject it, and if someone wants to accept it, it should not prevent him or fight against him. If someone does this, then it is the duty of Islam to fight him until either he is killed or until he declares his submission.

* * *

When writers with defeatist and apologetic mentalities write about

"**Jihaad** in Islam," trying to remove this 'blot' from Islam, then they are mixing up two things: first, that this religion forbids the imposition of its belief by force, as is clear from the verse,

لَآ إِكۡرَاهَ فِى ٱلدِّينِۖ

***"There is no compulsion in religion"*** *(2:256)*

while on the other hand it tries to annihilate all those political and material powers which stand between people and Islam, which force one people to bow before another people and prevent them from accepting the sovereignty of God. These two principles have no relation to one another nor is there room to mix them. In spite of this, these defeatist — type people try to mix the two aspects and want to confine **Jihaad** to what today is called 'defensive war'. The Islamic **Jihaad** has no relationship to modern warfare, either in its causes or in the way in which it is conducted. The causes of Islamic **Jihaad** should be sought in the very nature of Islam and its role in the world, in its high principles, which have been given to it by God and for the implementation of which God appointed the Prophet — peace be on him — as His Messenger and declared him to be the last of all prophets and messengers.

This religion is really a universal declaration of the freedom of man from servitude to other men and from servitude to his own desires, which is also a form of human servitude; it is a declaration that sovereignty belongs to God alone and that He is the Lord of all the worlds. It means a challenge to all kinds and forms of systems which are based on the concept of the sovereignty of man; in other words, where man has usurped the Divine attribute. Any system in which the final decisions are referred to human beings, and in which the sources of all authority are human, deifies human beings by designating others than God as lords over men. This declaration means that the usurped authority of God be returned to Him and the usurpers be thrown out — those who by themselves devise laws for others to follow, thus elevating themselves to the status of lords and reducing others to the status of slaves. In short, to proclaim the authority and sovereignty of God means to eliminate all human kingship and to announce the rule of the Sustainer of the universe over the entire earth. In the words of the Qur'an:

وَهُوَ ٱلَّذِى فِى ٱلسَّمَآءِ إِلَٰهٌ وَفِى ٱلۡأَرۡضِ

***"He alone is God in the heavens and in the earth."***
*(43:84)*

إِنِ الْحُكْمُ إِلَّا لِلَّهِ ۚ أَمَرَ أَلَّا تَعْبُدُوا إِلَّا إِيَّاهُ ۚ ذَٰلِكَ الدِّينُ الْقَيِّمُ

***"The command belongs to God alone, He commands you not to worship anyone except Him. This the right way of life.*** *(12:40)*

قُلْ يَا أَهْلَ الْكِتَابِ تَعَالَوْا إِلَىٰ كَلِمَةٍ سَوَاءٍ بَيْنَنَا وَبَيْنَكُمْ أَلَّا نَعْبُدَ إِلَّا اللَّهَ
وَلَا نُشْرِكَ بِهِ شَيْئًا وَلَا يَتَّخِذَ بَعْضُنَا بَعْضًا أَرْبَابًا مِّن دُونِ اللَّهِ ۚ فَإِن تَوَلَّوْا
فَقُولُوا اشْهَدُوا بِأَنَّا مُسْلِمُونَ ﴿٦٤﴾

***"Say: O People of the Book, come to what is common between us: that we will not worship an one except God, and will not associate anything with Him and will not take lords from among ourselves besides God: and it they turn away then tell them to bear witness that we are those who have submitted to God.*** *(3: 64)*

The way to establish God's rule on earth is not that some consecrated people the — priests — be given the authority to rule, as was the case with the rule of the Church, nor that some spokesmen of God become rulers, as is the case in a 'theocracy' To establish God's rule mean,. His laws be enforced and that the final decision in a affairs be according to these laws.

The establishing of the dominion of God on earth, the abolishing of the dominion of man, the taking away of sovereignty from the usurper to revert it to God, and the bringing about of the enforcement of the Divine Law (**Shari'ah**) and the abolition of man — made laws cannot be achieved only through preaching. Those who have usurped the authority of God and are oppressing God's creatures are not going to give up their power merely through preaching; if it had been so, the task of establishing God's religion in the world would have been very easy for the Prophets of God! This is contrary to the evidence from the history of the Prophets and the story of the struggle of the true religion, spread over generations.

This universal declaration of the freedom of man on the earth from every authority except that of God, and the declaration that sovereignty is God's alone and that He is the Lord of the universe, is not merely a theoretical, philosophical and passive proclamation. It is a positive, practical and dynamic message with a view to bringing about the implementation of the **Shari'ah** of God and actually freeing people from their servitude to other men to bring them into the service of God, the One without associates. This cannot be attained unless both 'preaching' and 'the movement' are used. This is so because appropriate means are needed to meet any and every practical situation.

Because this religion proclaims the freedom of man on the earth from all authority except that of God, it is confronted in every period of human history — yesterday, today, or tomorrow — with obstacles of beliefs and concepts, physical power, and the obstacles of political, social, economic, racial and class structures. In addition, corrupted beliefs and superstitions become mixed with this religion, working side by side with it and taking root in peoples' hearts.

If through 'preaching' beliefs and ideas are confronted, through 'the movement' material obstacles are tackled. Foremost among these is that political power which rests on a complex yet interrelated ideological, racial, class, social and economic support. Thus these two — preaching and the movement — united, confront 'the human situation' with all the necessary methods. For the achievement of the freedom of man on earth — of all mankind throughout the earth — it is necessary that these two methods should work side by side. This is a very important point and cannot be overemphasized.

This religion is not merely a declaration of the freedom of the Arabs, nor is its message confined to the Arabs. It addresses itself to the whole of mankind, and its sphere of work is the whole earth. God is the Sustainer not merely of the Arabs, nor is His providence limited to those who believe in the faith of Islam. God is the Sustainer of the whole world. This religion wants to bring back the whole world to its Sustainer and free it from servitude to anyone other than God. In the sight of Islam, the real servitude is following laws devised by someone, and this is that servitude which in Islam is reserved for God alone. Anyone who serves someone other than God in this sense is outside God's religion, although he may claim to profess this religion. The Prophet — peace be on him — clearly stated that, according to the **Shari'ah**, 'to obey' is 'to worship'. Taking this meaning of worship, when the Jews and Christians 'disobeyed' God, they became like those who 'associate others with God'.

Tirmidhi has reported on the authority of 'Adi bin Hatim that when the Prophet's message reached him, he ran away to Syria (he had accepted Christianity before the Prophet's time), but his sister and some of the people of his tribe became prisoners of war. The Prophet — peace be on him — treated his sister kindly and gave her some gifts. She went back to her brother and invited him to Islam, and advised him to visit the Prophet — peace be on him. 'Adi agreed to this. The people were very anxious to see him come to Medina. When he came into the presence of the Prophet, he was wearing a silver cross. The Prophet — peace be on him — was reciting the verse. "They (the People of the Book) have taken their rabbis and priests as lords other than God". 'Adi reports: "I said, 'They do not worship their priests." God's Messenger replied, "Whatever their priests and rabbis call permissible, they accept as permissible; whatever they declare as forbidden, they consider as forbidden, and thus they worship them"

This explanation of the above verse by the Prophet — peace be on him — makes it clear that obedience to laws and judgments is a sort of worship, and anyone who does this is considered out of this religion. It is taking some men as lords over others, while this religion has come to annihilate such practices, and it declares that all the people of the earth should become free of servitude to anyone other than God.

If the actual life of human beings is found to be different from this declaration of freedom, then it becomes incumbent upon Islam to enter the field with preaching as well as the movement, and to strike hard at all those political powers which force people to bow before them and which rule over them, unmindful of the commandments of God, and which prevent people from listening to the preaching and accepting the belief if they wish to do so. After annihilating the tyrannical force, whether it be in a political or a racial form, or in the form of class distinctions within the same race, Islam establishes a new social, economic and political system, in which the concept of the freedom of man is applied in practice.

It is not the intention of Islam to force its beliefs on people, but Islam is not merely 'belief'. As we have pointed out, Islam is a declaration of the freedom of man from servitude to other men. Thus it strives from the beginning to abolish all those systems and governments which are based on the rule of man over men and the servitude of one human being to another. When Islam releases people from this political pressure and presents to them its spiritual message, appealing to their reason, it gives them complete freedom to accept or not to accept its beliefs. However, this freedom does not mean that they can make their desires their gods, or that they can choose to remain in the servitude of other human beings, making some men lords over others. Whatever system is to be established in the world ought to be on the authority of God, deriving its laws from Him alone. Then every individual is free, under the protection of this universal system, to adopt any belief he wishes to adopt. This is the only way in which 'the religion' can be purified for God alone. The word 'religion' includes more than belief; 'religion' actually means a way of life, and in Islam this is based on belief. But in an Islamic system there is room for all kinds of people to follow their own beliefs, while obeying the laws of the country which are themselves based on the Divine authority.

Anyone who understands this particular character of this religion will also understand the place of **Jihaad bis saif** (striving through fighting), which is to clear the way for striving through preaching in the application of the Islamic movement. He will understand that Islam is not a 'defensive movemerit' in the narrow sense which today is technically called a 'defensive war.' This narrow meaning is ascribed to it by those who are under the pressure of circumstances and are defeated by the wily attacks of the orientalists, who distort the concept of Islamic **Jihaad**. It was a movement to wipe out tyranny and to introduce true freedom to mankind, using resources according to the actual human situation, and it had definite stages, for each of which it utilized new methods.

If we insist on calling Islamic **Jihaad** a defensive movement, then we must change the meaning of the word 'defence' and mean by it 'the defence of man against all those elements which limit his freedom. These elements take the form of beliefs and concepts, as well as of political systems, based on economic, racial or class distinctions. When Islam first came into existence, the world was full of such systems, and the present — day ***Jahiliyyah***also has various kinds of such systems. When we take this broad meaning of the word 'defence', we understand the true character of Islam, and that it is a universal proclamation of the freedom of man from servitude to other men, the establishment of the sovereignty of God and His Lordship throughout the world, the end of man's arrogance and selfishness, and the implementation of the rule of the Divine **Shari'ah** in human affairs.

As to persons who attempt to defend the concept of Islamic **Jihaad** by interpreting it in the narrow sense of the current concept of defensive war, and who do research to prove that the battles fought in Islamic **Jihaad** were all for the defence of the homeland of Islam — some of them considering the homeland of Islam to be just the Arabian peninsula — against the aggression of neighbouring powers, they lack understanding of the nature of Islam and its primary aim. Such anattempt is nothing but a product of a mind defeated by the present difficult conditions and by the attacks of the treacherous orientalists on the Islamic **Jihaad**.

Can anyone say that if Abu Bakr, 'Umar or Othman had been satisfied that the Roman and Persian powers were not going to attack the Arabian peninsula, they would not have striven to spread the message of Islam throughout the world? How could the message of Islam have spread when it faced such material obstacles as the political system of the state, the socio — economic system based on races and classes, and behind all these, the military power of the government?

It would be naive to assume that a call is raised to free the whole of humankind throughout the earth, and it is ,confined to preaching and exposition. Indeed, it strives through preaching and exposition when there is freedom of communication and when people are free from all these influences, as "There is no compulsion in religion; but when the abovementioned obstacles and practical difficulties are put in its way, it has no recourse but to remove them by force so that when it is addressed to peoples' hearts and minds they are free to accept or reject it with an open mind.

Since the objective of the message of Islam is a decisive declaration of man's freedom, not merely on the philosophical plane but also in the actual conditions of life, it must employ **Jihaad**. It is immaterial whether the homeland of Islam — in the true Islamic sense, **Dar ul-Islam** — is in a condition of peace or whether it is threatened by its neighbours. When Islam strives for peace, its objective is not that superficial peace which requires that only that part of the earth where the followers of Islam are residing remain secure . The peace which Islam desires is that the religion (i.e. the Law of the society) be purified for God, that the obedience of all people be for God alone, and that some people should not be lords over others. After the period of the Prophet — peace be on him — only the final stages of the movement of **Jihaad** are to be followed; the initial or middle stages are not applicable. They have ended, and as Ibn-Qayyim states, "Thus, after the revelation of the chapter 'Bra't', the unbelievers were of three kinds: adversaries in war, people with treaties, and **Dhimmies**. The people with treaties eventually became Muslims, so there were only two kinds left:, people at war and **Dhimmies**. The people at war were always afraid of him. Now the people of the whole world were of three kinds: one, the Muslims who believed in him: two, those with whom he had peace (and from the previous sentence we understand that they were **Dhimmies**); and three, the opponents who kept fighting him."

These are the logical positions consonant with the character and purposes of this religion, and not what is understood by the people who are defeated by present conditions and by the attacks of the treacherous orientalists..

God held back Muslims from fighting in Mecca and in the early period of their migration to Medina, and told them, "Restrain your hands, and establish regular prayers, and pay Zakat". Next, they were permitted to fight: — Permission to fight is given to those against whom war is made, because they are oppressed, and God is able to help them. These are the people who were expelled from their homes without cause. The next stage came when the Muslims were commanded to fight those who fight them: — Fight in the cause of God against those who fight you." And finally, war was declared against all the polytheists: "And fight against all the polytheists, as they all fight against you; "Fight against those among the People of the Book who do not believe in God and the Last Day, who do not forbid what God and His Messenger have forbidden, and who do not consider the true religion as their religion, until they are subdued and pay Jizyah". Thus, according to the explanation by Imam Ibn Qayyim, the Muslims were first restrained from fighting; then they were permitted to fight; then they were commanded to fight against the aggressors; and finally they were commanded to fight against all the polytheists.

With these verses from the Qur'an and with many Traditions of the Prophet — peace be on him — in praise of **Jihaad**, and with the entire history of Islam, which is full of **Jihaad**, the heart of every Muslim rejects that explanation of **Jihaad** invented by those people whose minds have accepted defeat under unfavourable conditions and under the attacks on Islamic **Jihaad** by the shrewd orientalists.

What kind of a man is it who, after listening to the commandment of God and the Traditions of the Prophet — peace be on him — and after reading about the events which occurred during the Islamic **Jihaad**, still thinks that it is a temporary injunction related to transient conditions and that it is concerned only with the defence of the borders?

In the verse giving permission to fight, God has informed the Believers that the life of this world is such that checking one group of people by another is the law of God, so that the earth may be cleansed of corruption. — Permission to fight is given to those against whom war is made, because they are oppressed, and God is able to help them. These are the people who were expelled from their homes without cause, except that they said that our Lord is God. **Had God not checked one people by another, then surely synagogues and churches and mosques would have been pulled down, where the name of God is remembered often."** Thus, this struggle is not a temporary phase but an eternal state — an eternal state, as truth and falsehood cannot co — exist on this earth. Whenever Islam stood up with the universal declaration that God's Lordship should be established over the entire earth and that men should become free from servitude to other men, the usurpers of God's authority on earth have struck out against it fiercely and have never tolerated it. It became incumbent upon Islam to strike back and release man throughout the earth from the grip of these usurpers. The eternal struggle for the freedom of man will continue until the religion is purified for God.

The command to refrain from fighting during the Meccan period was a temporary stage in a long journey. The same reason was operative during the early days of Hijra, but after these early stages, the reason for **Jihaad** was not merely to defend Medina. Indeed, its defence was necessary, but this was not the ultimate aim. The aim was to protect the resources and the centre of the movement — the . movement for freeing mankind and demolishing the obstacles which prevented mankind from attaining this freedom.

The reasons for refraining from fighting during the Meccan period are easily understood. In Mecca preaching was permitted. The Messenger — peace be on him — was under the protection of the Banu Hashim and hence he had the opportunity to declare his message openly; he had the freedom to speak to individuals as to groups and to appeal to their hearts and minds. There was no organized political power which could prevent him from preaching and prevent people from listening. At this stage there was no need for the use of force. Besides this, there were other reasons and I have detailed these reasons in my commentary, **In the Shades of the Qur'an**, in explanation of the verse,

أَلَمْ تَرَ إِلَى الَّذِينَ قِيلَ لَهُمْ كُفُّوا أَيْدِيَكُمْ وَأَقِيمُوا الصَّلَوٰةَ وَآتُوا الزَّكَوٰةَ

**"Have you seen the people to whom it was said, 'Restrain your hands, and establish regular prayers, and pay Zakat?"** (4:77) It may be useful to reproduce parts of this explanation here.

"A reason for prohibiting the use of force during the Meccan period may have been that this was a stage of training and preparation in a particular environment, for a particular nation and under particular conditions. Under these circumstances, an important factor in training and preparation was to train the individual Arab to be patient under oppression to himself or to those he loved, to conquer his pride, and not to make personal revenge or revenge for one's dear ones the purpose of one's life. Training was also needed so that he could learn control of his nerves, not lose his temper at the first provocation — as was his temperament — nor get excited at the first impulse, but so that he could develop dignity and composure in his temperament and in his action. He was to be trained to follow the discipline of a community which is under the direction of a leader, and to refer to this leader in every matter and to obey his injunctions, even though they might be against his habit or taste. The aim was to develop individuals of high character who would constitute the Muslim community, who would follow the directions of the leader, and who would be civilized and progressive, free of wild habits and tribalism.

"Another reason for it may have been that the Quraish were proud of their lineage and honor, and in such an environment only persuasion could be most appealing and effective. At this stage, fighting would have resulted in kindling the fires of revenge. There was already much tribal warfare based on blood feuds, such as the wars of Dahis, Gabra and Basus, which continued for years and annihilated tribe after tribe. If blood feuds were to become associated in their minds with Islam, then this impression would never have been removed. Consequently, Islam, instead of being a call toward the true religion, would have become an unending sequence of tribal feuds and its basic teachings would have been forgotten at the very beginning.

"Another reason may have been to avoid sowing the seed of discord and bloodshed in every household. At that time, there was no organized government which was torturing and persecuting the Believers; the Believer was persecuted, tortured and 'taught a lesson' by his own patrons. Under these circumstances, permission to fight would have meant that every house would have become a battlefield. The people would have said 'So, this is Islam'! In fact, this was said about Islam, even though fighting was not permitted. During the season when the people of Arabia came to Mecca for pilgrimage and commerce, the Quraish would have gone to them and would have said, 'Muhammad is not only dividing his nation and his tribe; he is even dividing sons from fathers! What kind of a thing is this which incites the son to kill his father, the slave to kill his master, in every house and in every locality?"

"Another reason may have been that God knew that a great majority of those who persecuted and tortured the early Muslims would one day become the loyal soldiers of Islam, even its great leaders. Was not 'Umar Ibn al-Khattab one of them?

"Another reason may have been that the sense of honor of the Arabs, especially in a tribal framework, comes to the help of the person who is persecuted yet does not concede defeat, especially if the persecuted are honored by the people. Several such incidents can be quoted to support this thesis. When Abu Bakr, who was an honorable man, left Mecca in order to migrate to some other place, Ibn al-Daghna could not bear it and restrained him from leaving because he considered it a disgrace to the

Arabs; he offered Abu Bakr his own protection. The best example of such an incident is the tearing up of the contract under which the Banu Hashim were confined to the Valley of Abu Talib when the period of their hunger and privation seemed unreasonably long. This chivalry was a peculiarity of the Arabs, while in ancient 'civilizations' which were accustomed to seeing people humiliated, those who suffered and were persecuted were laughed at, ridiculed and treated with contempt, and the oppressor and the tyrant were respected.

"Another reason may have been that the Muslims were few in number and they lived only in M ecca, as the message of Islam had not reached other parts of Arabia or had reached. only as hearsay. Other tribes considered it as a domestic quarrel of the Quraish; they were watching for the outcome of this struggle. Under these circumstances, if fighting had been allowed, this limited warfare would have resulted in the complete annihilation of the Muslims; even if they had killed a great number of their opponents, they would still have been completely annihilated. Idolatry would have continued and the dawn of the Islamic system would never have arrived and would never have reached its zenith, while Islam is revealed to be a practical way of life for all mankind".

In the early Medinite period fighting was also prohibited. The reason for this was that the Prophet — peace be on him — had signed a pact with the Jews of Medina and with the unbelieving Arabs in and around Medina, an action which was necessary at this stage.

First, there was an open opportunity for preaching and persuasion. There was no political power to circumscribe this freedom; the whole population accepted the new Muslim state and agreed upon the leadership of the Prophet — peace be on him — in all political matters. In the pact it was agreed by all parties that no one would make a treaty of peace or declare war or establish relations with any outsider without the express permission of the Prophet — peace be on him. Thus, the real power in Medina was in the hands of Muslim leadership. The doors were also open for preaching Islam and there was freedom of belief.

Secondly, at this stage the Prophet — peace be on him — wanted to conserve all his efforts to combat the Quraish, whose relentless opposition was a great obstacle in spreading Islam to other tribes which were waiting to see the final outcome of the struggle between the two groups of the Quraish. That is why the Prophet — peace be on him — hastened to send scouting parties in various directions. The first such party was commanded by Hamza bin Abdul Muttalib, and it went out during the month of Ramadan, only six months after the Immigration.

After this, there were other scouting parties, one during the ninth month after Hijra, the next in the thirteenth month, the third sixteen months after Hijra, and in the seventeenth month he sent a party under the leadership of Abdullah bin Jahash. This party encountered some resistance and some blood was shed. This occurred during the month of Rajab, which was considered a sacred month. The following verse of Chapter Baqara refers to it:

يَسْـَٔلُونَكَ عَنِ الشَّهْرِ الْحَرَامِ قِتَالٍ فِيهِ ۖ قُلْ قِتَالٌ فِيهِ كَبِيرٌ ۖ وَصَدٌّ عَنْ
سَبِيلِ اللّٰهِ وَكُفْرٌۢ بِهٖ وَالْمَسْجِدِ الْحَرَامِ ۚ وَإِخْرَاجُ أَهْلِهٖ مِنْهُ أَكْبَرُ عِنْدَ اللّٰهِ ۚ
وَالْفِتْنَةُ أَكْبَرُ مِنَ الْقَتْلِ ۗ

***"They ask you about fighting in the sacred months. Say: Fighting in them is a great sin, but to prevent people from the way of God, and to reject God, and to stop people from visiting the Sacred Mosque, and to expel people from their homes are a much greater sin, and oppression is worse than killing." (2:217)***

During Ramadan of the same year, the Battle of Badr took place, and in Chapter Anfal this battle was reviewed.

If this stage of the Islamic movement is viewed in proper perspective, then there is no room to say that the basic aim of the Islamic movement was 'defensive' in the narrow sense which some people ascribe to it today, defeated by the attacks of the treacherous orientalists!

Those who look for causes of a defensive nature in the history of the expansion of Islam are caught by the aggressive attacks of the orientalists at a time when Muslims possess neither glory nor do they possess Islam. However, by God's grace, there are those who are standing firm on the issue that Islam is a universal declaration of the freedom of man on the earth from every authority except God's authority, and that the religion ought to be purified for God; and they keep writing concerning, the Islamic **Jihaad**.

But the Islamic movement does not need any arguments taken from the literature, as it stands on the clear verses of the Qur'an:

فَلْيُقَاتِلْ فِي سَبِيلِ اللّٰهِ الَّذِينَ يَشْرُونَ الْحَيٰوةَ الدُّنْيَا بِالْاٰخِرَةِ ۚ وَمَنْ يُقَاتِلْ فِي
سَبِيلِ اللّٰهِ فَيُقْتَلْ أَوْ يَغْلِبْ فَسَوْفَ نُؤْتِيهِ أَجْرًا عَظِيمًا ﴿٧٤﴾ وَمَا لَكُمْ لَا تُقَاتِلُونَ

فِي سَبِيلِ اللَّهِ وَالْمُسْتَضْعَفِينَ مِنَ الرِّجَالِ وَالنِّسَاءِ وَالْوِلْدَانِ الَّذِينَ يَقُولُونَ رَبَّنَا
أَخْرِجْنَا مِنْ هَٰذِهِ الْقَرْيَةِ الظَّالِمِ أَهْلُهَا وَاجْعَل لَّنَا مِن لَّدُنكَ وَلِيًّا وَاجْعَل
لَّنَا مِن لَّدُنكَ نَصِيرًا ٧٥

*"They ought to fight in the way of God who have sold the life of this world for the life of the Hereafter; and whoever fights in the way of God and is killed or becomes victorious, to him shall We give a great reward. Why should not you fight in the way of God for those men, women and children who have been oppressed because they are weak and who call 'Our Lord! Take us out of this place whose people are oppressors, and raise for us an ally, and send for us a helper'.*
*(4:74-76)*

قُل لِّلَّذِينَ كَفَرُوا إِن يَنتَهُوا يُغْفَرْ لَهُم مَّا قَدْ سَلَفَ وَإِن يَعُودُوا فَقَدْ مَضَتْ
سُنَّتُ الْأَوَّلِينَ ٣٨ وَقَاتِلُوهُمْ حَتَّىٰ لَا تَكُونَ فِتْنَةٌ وَيَكُونَ الدِّينُ كُلُّهُ لِلَّهِ فَإِنِ
انتَهَوْا فَإِنَّ اللَّهَ بِمَا يَعْمَلُونَ بَصِيرٌ ٣٩ وَإِن تَوَلَّوْا فَاعْلَمُوا أَنَّ اللَّهَ مَوْلَاكُمْ نِعْمَ الْمَوْلَىٰ
وَنِعْمَ النَّصِيرُ ٤٠

*"Say to the unbelievers that if they refrain, then whatever they have done before will be forgiven them; but if they turn back, then they know what happened to earlier nations. And fight against them until there is no oppression and the religion is wholly for God. But if they refrain, then God is watching over their actions. But if they do not, then know that God is your Ally and He is your Helper."* *(8:38-40)*

قَاتِلُوا الَّذِينَ لَا يُؤْمِنُونَ بِاللَّهِ وَلَا بِالْيَوْمِ الْآخِرِ وَلَا يُحَرِّمُونَ مَا حَرَّمَ اللَّهُ
وَرَسُولُهُ وَلَا يَدِينُونَ دِينَ الْحَقِّ مِنَ الَّذِينَ أُوتُوا الْكِتَابَ حَتَّىٰ يُعْطُوا الْجِزْيَةَ
عَن يَدٍ وَهُمْ صَاغِرُونَ ٢٩ وَقَالَتِ الْيَهُودُ عُزَيْرٌ ابْنُ اللَّهِ وَقَالَتِ النَّصَارَى
الْمَسِيحُ ابْنُ اللَّهِ ذَٰلِكَ قَوْلُهُم بِأَفْوَاهِهِمْ يُضَاهِئُونَ قَوْلَ الَّذِينَ كَفَرُوا مِن
قَبْلُ قَاتَلَهُمُ اللَّهُ أَنَّىٰ يُؤْفَكُونَ ٣٠ اتَّخَذُوا أَحْبَارَهُمْ وَرُهْبَانَهُمْ أَرْبَابًا

مِّنْ دُوْنِ اللّٰهِ وَالْمَسِيْحَ ابْنَ مَرْيَمَ ۚ وَمَآ اُمِرُوْٓا اِلَّا لِيَعْبُدُوْٓا اِلٰهًا وَّاحِدًا ۚ لَآ اِلٰهَ
اِلَّا هُوَ ۭ سُبْحٰنَهٗ عَمَّا يُشْرِكُوْنَ ﴿٣١﴾ يُرِيْدُوْنَ اَنْ يُّطْفِـُٔوْا نُوْرَ اللّٰهِ بِاَفْوَاهِهِمْ وَيَاْبَى
اللّٰهُ اِلَّآ اَنْ يُّتِمَّ نُوْرَهٗ وَلَوْ كَرِهَ الْكٰفِرُوْنَ ﴿٣٢﴾

***"Fight against those among the People of the Book who do not believe in God and the Last Day, who do not forbid what God and His messenger have forbidden, and who do not consider the true religion as their way of life, until they are subdued and pay Jizyah. The Jews say: 'Ezra is the Son of God', and the Christians say: 'The Messiah is the Son of God'. These are mere sayings from their mouths, following those who preceded them and disbelieved. God will assail them; how they are perverted! They have taken their rabbis and priests as lords other that God, and the Messiah, son of Mary; and they were commanded to worship none but One God. There is no deity but He, glory be to Him above what they associate with Him! They desire to extinguish God's light with their mouths, and God intends to perfect His light, although the unbelievers may be in opposition" (9: 29 — 32)***

The reasons for **Jihaad** which have been described in the above verses are these: to establish God's authority in the earth; to arrange human affairs according to the true guidance provided by God; to abolish all the Satanic forces and Satanic systems of life; to end the lordship of one man over others, since all men are creatures of God and no one has the authority to make them his servants or to make arbitrary laws for them. These reasons are sufficient for proclaiming **Jihaad**. However, one should always keep in mind that there is no compulsion in religion; that is, once the people are free from the lordship of men, the law governing civil affairs will be purely that of God, while no one will be forced to change his beliefs and accept Islam.

The **Jihaad** of Islam is to secure complete freedom for every man throughout the world by releasing him from servitude to other human beings so that he may serve his God, Who is One and Who has no associates. This is in itself a sufficient reason for **Jihaad**. These were the only reasons in the hearts of Muslim warriors. If they had been asked the question, "Why are you fighting?" none would have answered, "My country is in danger; I am fighting for its defence" or "The Persians and the Romans have come upon us", or, "We want to extend our dominion and want more spoils:

They would have answered the same as Raba'i bin 'Amer, Huzaifa bin Muhsin and Mughira bin Sh'uba answered the Persian general Rustum when he asked them one by one during three successive days preceding the battle of Qadisiyyah, "For what purpose have you come?" Their answer was the same: "God has sent us to bring anyone who wishes from servitude to men into the service of God alone, from the narrowness of this world into the vastness of this world and the Hereafter, and from the tyranny of religions into the justice of Islam. God raised a Messenger for this purpose to teach His creatures His way. If anyone accepts this way of life, we turn back and give his country back to him, and we fight with those who rebel until we are martyred or become victorious".

These are the reasons inherent in the very nature of this religion. Similarly, its proclamation of universal freedom, its practical way of combatting actual human conditions with appropriate methods, its developing new resources at various stages, is also inherent in its message from the very beginning — and not because of any threat of aggression against Islamic lands or against the Muslims residing in them. The reason for **Jihaad** exists in the nature of its message and in the actual conditions it finds in human societies, and not merely in the necessity for defence, which may be temporary and of limited extent. A Muslim fights with his wealth and his person "in the way of God" for the sake of these values in which neither personal gain nor greed is a motive for him.

Before a Muslim steps into the battlefield, he has already fought a great battle within himself against Satan — against his own desires and ambitions, his personal interests and inclinations, the interests of his family and of his nation; against which is not from Islam; against every obstacle which comes into the way of worshipping God and the implementation of the Divine authority on earth, returning this authority to God and taking it away from the rebellious usurpers.

Those who say that Islamic **Jihaad** was merely for the defence of the 'homeland of Islam' diminish the greatness of the Islamic way of life and consider it less important than their 'homeland'. This is not the Islamic point of view, and their view is a creation of the modern age and is completely alien to Islamic consciousness. What is acceptable to Islamic consciousness is its belief, the way of life which this belief prescribes, and the society which lives according to this way of life. The soil of the homeland has in itself no value or weight. From the Islamic point of view, the only value which the soil can achieve is because on that soil God's authority is established and God's guidance is followed; and thus it becomes a fortress for the belief, a place for its way of life to be entitled the 'homeland of Islam', a center for the movement for the total freedom of man.

Of course, in that case the defence of the 'homeland of Islam' is the defence of the Islamic beliefs, the Islamic way of life, and the Islamic community. However, its defence is not the ultimate objective of the Islamic movement of **Jihaad** but is a means of establishing the Divine authority within it so that it becomes the headquarters for the movement of Islam, which is then to be carried throughout the earth to the whole of mankind, as the object of this religion is all humanity and its sphere of action is the whole earth.

As we have described earlier, there are many practical obstacles in establishing God's rule on earth, such as the power of the state, the social system and traditions and, in general, the whole human environment. Islam uses force only to remove these obstacles so that there may not remain any wall between Islam and individual human beings, and so that it may address their hearts and minds after releasing them from these material obstacles, and then leave them free to choose to accept or reject it.

We ought not to be deceived or embarrassed by the attacks of the orientalists on the origin of **Jihaad**, nor lose selfconfidence under the pressure of present conditions and the weight of the great powers of the world to such an extent that we try to find reasons for Islamic **Jihaad** outside the nature of this religion, and try to show that it was a defensive measure under temporary conditions. The need for **Jihaad** remains, and will continue to remain, whether these conditions exist or not!

In pondering over historical events, we should not neglect the aspects inherent in the nature of this religion, its declaration of universal freedom, and its practical method. We ought not to confuse these with temporary needs of defence.

No doubt this religion must defend itself against aggressors. Its very existence in the form of a general declaration of the universal Lordship of God and of the freedom of man from servitude to any being other than God, and its organizing a movement under a new leadership other than the existing ***jahili*** leadership, and its creating a distinct and permanent society based on the Divine authority and submission to One God, is sufficient cause for the surrounding ***jahili*** society, which is based on human authority in some form or another, to, rise against it for its own preservation and for the suppression of Islam. Clearly, under these conditions, the newly organized Islamic community will have to prepare itself for defence. These conditions inevitably occur and come into existence simultaneously with the advent of Islam in any society. There is no question of Islam's liking or disliking such a situation, as the struggle is imposed upon Islam; this is a natural struggle between two systems which cannot co — exist for long. This is a fact which cannot be denied, and hence Islam has no choice but to defend itself against aggression.

But there is another fact which is much more important than this fact. It is in the very nature of Islam to take initiative for freeing the human beings throughout the earth from servitude to anyone other than God; and so it cannot be restricted within any geographic or racial limits, leaving all mankind on the whole earth in evil, in chaos and in servitude to lords other than God.

It may happen that the enemies of Islam may consider it expedient not to take any action against Islam, if Islam leaves them alone in their geographical boundaries to continue the lordship of some men over others and does not extend its message and its declaration of universal freedom within their domain. But Islam cannot agree to this unless they submit to its authority by paying jizyah, which will be a guarantee that they have opened their doors for the preaching of Islam and will not put any obstacle in its way through the power of the state.

This is the character of this religion and this is its function, as it is a declaration of the Lordship of God and the freedom of man from servitude to anyone other than God, for all people.

There is a great difference between this concept of Islam and the other, which considers it confined to geographical and racial limits, and does not take any action except out of fear of aggression. In the latter case, all its inherent dynamism is lost.

To understand the dynamism of Islam with clarity and depth, it is necessary to remember that Islam is a way of life for man prescribed by God. It is not a man — made system, nor an ideology of a group of people, nor a way of life peculiar to a given race. We cannot talk about external reasons for **Jihaad** unless we overlook this great truth and unless we forget that the fundamental question here is the sovereignty of God and the obedience of His creatures; it is impossible for a person to remember this great truth and still search for other reasons for Islamic **Jihaad**.

The true estimate of the difference between the concept that war was forced upon Islam by ***Jahiliyyah*** because its very nature demanded that ***jahili*** societies would attack it, and the concept that Islam takes the initiative and enters into this struggle, cannot be made in the early stages of its movement.

In the early stages of the Islamic movement it is difficult to discriminate between these two concepts, because in either case Islam will have to do battle. However, in the final stages, when the initial battles are won, the two concepts make a great difference — a great difference in understanding the purposes and the significance of the Islamic message. And here lies the danger.

There is also a great difference in the idea that Islam is a Divinely — ordained way of life and in the idea that it is a geographically — bounded system. According to the first idea, Islam came into this world to establish God's rule on God's earth, to invite all people toward the worship of God, and to make a concrete reality of its message in the form of a Muslim community in which individuals are free from servitude to men and have gathered together under servitude to God and follow only the **Shari'ah** of God. This Islam has a right to remove all those obstacles which are in its path so that it may address human reason and intuition with no interference and opposition from political systems. According to the second idea, Islam is merely a national system which has a right to take up arms only when its homeland is attacked.

In the case of either concept, Islam has to strive and to struggle; but its purposes and its results are entirely different, both conceptually and practically.

Indeed, Islam has the right to take the initiative. Islam is not a heritage of any particular race or country; this is God's religion and it is for the whole world. It has the right to destroy all obstacles in the form of institutions and traditions which limit man's freedom of choice. It does not attack individuals nor does it force them to accept its beliefs; it attacks institutions and traditions to release human beings from their poisonous influences, which distort human nature and which curtail human freedom.

It is the right of Islam to release mankind from servitude to human beings so that they may serve God alone, to give practical meaning to its declaration that God is the true Lord of all and that all men are free under Him. According to the Islamic concept and in actuality, God's rule on earth can be established only through the Islamic system, as it is the only system ordained by God for all human beings, whether they be rulers or ruled, black or white, poor or rich, ignorant or learned. Its law is uniform for all, and all human beings are equally responsible within it. In all other systems, human beings obey other human beings and follow man — made laws. Legislation is a Divine attribute; any person who concedes this right to such a claimant, whether he considers him Divine or not, has accepted him as Divine.

Islam is not merely a belief, so that it is enough merely to preach it. Islam, which is a way of life, takes practical steps to organize a movement for freeing man. Other societies do not give it any opportunity to organize its followers according to its own method, and hence it is the duty of Islam to annihilate all such systems, as they are obstacles in the way of universal freedom. Only in this manner can the way of life be wholly dedicated to God, so that neither any human authority nor the question of servitude remains, as is 'the case in all other systems which are based on man's servitude to man.

Those of our contemporary Muslim scholars who are defeated by the pressure of current conditions and the attacks of treacherous orientalists do not subscribe to this characteristic of Islam. The orientalists have painted a picture of Islam as a violent movement which imposed its belief upon people by the sword. These vicious orientalists know very well that this is not true, but by this method they try to distort the true motives of Islamic **Jihaad**. But our Muslim scholars, these defeated people, search for reasons of defensive with which to negate this accusation. They are ignorant of the nature of Islam and of its function, and that it has a right to take the initiative for human freedom.

These research scholars, with their defeated mentality, have adopted the Western concept of 'religion', which is merely a name for 'belief' in the heart, having no relation to the practical affairs of life, and therefore they conceive of religious war as a war to impose belief on peoples' hearts.

But this is not the case with Islam, as Islam is the way of life ordained by God for all mankind, and this way establishes the Lordship of God alone — that is, the sovereignty of God — and orders practical life in all its daily details. **Jihaad** in Islam is simply a name for striving to make this system of life dominant in the world. As far as belief is concerned, it clearly depends upon personal opinion, under the protection of a general system in which all obstacles to freedom of personal belief have been removed. Clearly this is an entirely different matter and throws a completely new light on the Islamic **Jihaad**.

Thus, wherever an Islamic community exists which is a concrete example of the Divinely — ordained system of life, it has a God — given right to step forward and take control of the political authority so that it may establish the Divine system on earth, while it leaves the matter of belief to individual conscience. When God restrained Muslims from **Jihaad** for a certain period, it was a question of strategy rather than of principle; this was a matter pertaining to the requirements of the movement and not to belief. Only in the light of this explanation can we understand those verses of the Holy Qur'an which are concerned with the various stages of this movement. In reading these verses, we should always keep in mind that one of their meanings is related to the particular stages of the development of Islam, while there is another general meaning which is related to the unchangeable and eternal message of Islam. We should not confuse these two aspects.

## *CHAPTER 5*

# LA ILAHA ILLA ALLAH — THE WAY OF LIFE OF ISLAM

'**La ilaha illa Allah**" — "There is no deity except Allah" — is the first part the Islamic declaration of faith, meaning that there is no one to be worshipped except God; **"Muhammadar Rasul Allah"** — "Muhammad is the Messenger of God; — is the second part, meaning that this worship is to be carried out according to the teaching of the Prophet — peace be on him.

A believing Muslim is one into whose heart this declaration has penetrated completely, as the other pillars of Islam and articles of faith are derivatives of it. Thus, belief in angels and God's Books and God's Messengers and the life hereafter and **al-Qadr** (the measurement of good and evil), and **al-Salat** (prayers), **al-Siyam** (fasting), **al-Zakat** (poor — due) and **al-Hajj** (pilgrimage), and the limits set by God of permissable and forbidden things, human affairs, laws, Islamic moral teachings, and so on, are all based on the foundation of worship of God, and the source of all these teachings is the person of the Prophet — peace be on him — through whom God has revealed to us.

A Muslim community is that which is a practical interpretation of the declaration of faith and all its charactaristics; and the society which does not translate into practice this faith and its charactaristics is not Muslim.

Thus the declaration of faith provides the foundation for a complete system of life for the Muslim community in all its details. This way of life cannot come into being without securing this foundation first. Similarly, if the system of life is constructed on some other foundation, or if other sources are mixed with this foundation, then that community cannot be considered Islamic. God says:

إِنِ الْحُكْمُ إِلَّا لِلَّهِ ۚ أَمَرَ أَلَّا تَعْبُدُوا إِلَّا إِيَّاهُ ۚ ذَٰلِكَ الدِّينُ الْقَيِّمُ

*"The command belongs to God alone. He commands you not to worship anyone except Him. This is the right way of life."* (12:40)

مَنْ يُطِعِ الرَّسُولَ فَقَدْ أَطَاعَ اللَّهَ ۖ

*"Whoever obeys the Prophet obeys God"* (4:80)

* * *

This concise and decisive declaration guides us in the basic questions of our religion and in its practical movement. First, it guides us to the nature of the Muslim community; second, it shows us the method of constructing such a community; third, it tells us how to confront ***jahili*** societies; and fourth, it determines the method by which Islam changes the conditions of human life. All these problems have always been and will remain of great importance in the various stages of the Islamic movement.

* * *

The distinctive feature of a Muslim community is this: that in all its affairs it is based on worship of God alone. The declaration of faith expresses this principle and determines its character; in beliefs, in devotional acts, and in rules and regulations this declaration takes a concrete form. A person who does not believe in the oneness of God does not worship God alone.

وَقَالَ اللَّهُ لَا تَتَّخِذُوا إِلَٰهَيْنِ اثْنَيْنِ ۖ إِنَّمَا هُوَ إِلَٰهٌ وَاحِدٌ ۖ فَإِيَّايَ فَارْهَبُونِ ﴿٥١﴾

وَلَهُ مَا فِي السَّمَاوَاتِ وَالْأَرْضِ وَلَهُ الدِّينُ وَاصِبًا ۚ أَفَغَيْرَ اللَّهِ تَتَّقُونَ ﴿٥٢﴾

*"Allah commands you not to take two gods. God is only One; hence fear Me. Whatever is in the heavens and the earth belongs to Him and follows His way. Will you then fear anyone other than God?'* (16: 51-52)

Anyone who performs devotional acts before someone other than God — in addition to Him or exclusively — does not worship God alone.

قُلْ إِنَّ صَلَاتِي وَنُسُكِي وَمَحْيَايَ وَمَمَاتِي لِلَّهِ رَبِّ الْعَالَمِينَ ﴿١٦٢﴾

لَا شَرِيكَ لَهُ ۖ وَبِذَٰلِكَ أُمِرْتُ وَأَنَا أَوَّلُ الْمُسْلِمِينَ ﴿١٦٣﴾

*"Say, my Salat (prayers), my acts of devciion, my life and my death, are for the Sustainer of the Worlds; He has no associate. I have been*

> ***commanded this, and I am the foremost to be among the submitters."*** *(6:162-163)*

Anyone who derives laws from a source other than God, in a way other than what He taught us through the Prophet — peace be on him — does not worship God alone.

أَمْ لَهُمْ شُرَكَٰٓؤُا شَرَعُوا لَهُمْ مِّنَ الدِّينِ مَا لَمْ يَأْذَنۢ بِهِ اللَّهُ

> ***"Are there associates of God who have made permissable for them in their religion that which God has not permitted?"*** *(42:21)*

وَمَآ ءَاتَىٰكُمُ الرَّسُولُ فَخُذُوهُ وَمَا نَهَىٰكُمْ عَنْهُ فَانْتَهُوا

> ***"Whatever the Prophet gives you, accept it, and whatever he prohibits you, refrain from it."*** *(59:7)*

This is the Muslim society. In this society, the beliefs and ideas of individuals, their devotional acts and religious observances, and their social system and their laws, are all based on submission to God alone. If this attitude is eliminated from any of these aspects, the whole of Islam is eliminated, as the first pillar of Islam — that is, the declaration, 'there is no deity except God, and Muhammad is the Messenger of God' — becomes eliminated.

Thus, and only thus, can this group become a Muslim group and the community which it organizes be Muslim. Before adopting this purity of attitude no group can be a Muslim group, and before organizing its system of life on this principle no society can be a Muslim society. The reason for this is that the first principle on which Islam is based, that is **"La ilaha illa Allah, Muhammadar Rasul Allah"**, is not established in respect to both its parts.

It is necessary, therefore, before thinking of establishing the Islamic social system and organizing a Muslim communiry, that one should give attention to purifying the hearts of people from the worship of anyone other than God, in the way we have described above. Only those whose hearts are so purified will come together to make a group, and only such a group of people, whose beliefs and concepts, whose devotional acts and laws, are completely free of servitude to anyone other than God can start a Muslim community. Anyone who wants to live an Islamic life will automatically enter into this community, and his belief, his acts of worship and the laws which he follows, will also be purified for God alone. In other words, he will be an embodiment of **"La ilaha illa Allah, Muhammadar**

Rasul Allah".

This was the manner in which the first Muslim group was formed which eventually developed into the first Muslim community. This is the only way in which any Muslim group is started and a Muslim community comes into being.

A Muslim community can come into existence only when individuals and groups of people reject servitude to anyone except God — in addition to Him or exclusively — and come into submission to God, Who has no associates, and decide that they will organize their scheme or life on the basis of this submission. From this a new community is born, emerging from within the old *jahili* society, which immediately confronts it with a new belief and a new way of life based on this belief, presenting a concrete embodiment of the creed, "There is no deity except God, and Muhammad is the Messenger of God".

The old *jahili* society may become submerged into the new Islamic society or it may not, and it may make peace with the Muslim society or may fight it. However, history tells us that the *jahili* society chooses to fight and not to make peace, attacking the vanguard of Islam at its very inception, whether it be a few individuals or whether it be groups, and even after this vanguard has become a well — established community. From Noah to Muhammad — peace be on them — without exception, this has been the course of events at every Islamic call.

It is clear, then, that a Muslim community cannot be formed or continue to exist until it attains sufficient power to confront the existing *jahili* society. This power must be at all levels; that is to say, the power of belief and concept, the power of training and moral character, the power to organize and sustain a community, and such physical power as is necessary, if not to dominate, at least to hold itself against the onslaught of the *jahili* society.

* * *

But what is the *jahili* society, and by what method does Islam confront it?

The *jahili* society is any society other than the Muslim society; and if we want a more specific definition, we may say that any society is a *jahili* society which does not dedicate itself to submission to God alone, in its beliefs and ideas, in its observances of worship, and in its legal regulations.

According to this definition, all the societies existing in the world today are *jahili*.

Included among these is the communist society, first because it denies the existence of God Most High and believes that the universe was created by 'matter' or by 'nature', while all man's activities and his history has been created by 'economics' or 'the means of production'; second, because the way of life it adopts is based on submission to the Communist Party and not to God. A proof of this is that in all communist countries the Communist Party has full control and leadership. Furthermore, the practical consequence of this ideology is that the basic needs of human beings are considered identical with those of animals, that is food and drink, clothing, shelter and sex. It deprives people of their spiritual needs, which differentiate human beings from animals. Foremost among these is belief in God and the freedom to adopt and to proclaim this faith. Similarly, it deprives people of their freedom to express individuality, which is a very special human characteristic. The individuality of a person is expressed in various ways, such as private property, the choice of work and the attainment of specialization in work, and expression in various art forms; and it distinguishes him from animals or from machines. The communist ideology and the communist system reduces the human being to the level of an animal or even to the level of a machine.

All idolatrous societies are also among the *jahili* societies. Such societies are found in India, Japan, the Philippines and Africa. Their *jahili* character consists first of the fact that they believe in other gods besides God, in addition to Him or without Him; second; they have constructed an elaborate system of devotional acts to propitiate these deities. Similarly, the laws and regulations which they follow are derived from sources other than Cod and His Law, whether these sources be priests or astrologers or magicians, the elders of the nation, or the secular institutions which formulate laws without regard to the Law of God, and which attain absolute authority in the name of the nation or a party or on some other basis, while absolute authority belongs to God alone, and this can be brought into action only in the way shown to us by the Prophets of God.

All Jewish and Christian societies today are also *jahili* societies. They have distorted the original beliefs and ascribe certain attributes of God to other beings. This association with God has taken many forms, such as the Sonship of God or the Trinity; sometimes it is expressed in a concept of God which is remote from the true reality of God.

وَقَالَتِ الْيَهُودُ عُزَيْرٌ ابْنُ اللَّهِ وَقَالَتِ النَّصَارَى الْمَسِيحُ ابْنُ اللَّهِ ۖ ذَٰلِكَ قَوْلُهُم
بِأَفْوَاهِهِمْ ۖ يُضَاهِئُونَ قَوْلَ الَّذِينَ كَفَرُوا مِن قَبْلُ ۚ قَاتَلَهُمُ اللَّهُ ۚ أَنَّىٰ
يُؤْفَكُونَ ﴿٣٠﴾

> *"The Jews say: Ezra is the Son of God', and the Christians say: "the Messiah is the Son of God.' These are mere sayings from their mouths, following those who preceded them and disbelieved. God will assail them: how they are per verted." (9:30)*

لَقَدْ كَفَرَ الَّذِينَ قَالُوا إِنَّ اللَّهَ ثَالِثُ ثَلَاثَةٍ ۘ وَمَا مِنْ إِلَٰهٍ إِلَّا إِلَٰهٌ وَاحِدٌ ۚ وَإِنْ
لَمْ يَنْتَهُوا عَمَّا يَقُولُونَ لَيَمَسَّنَّ الَّذِينَ كَفَرُوا مِنْهُمْ عَذَابٌ أَلِيمٌ ﴿٧٣﴾

> *"They rejected the truth who said; 'God is the third of three'. Indeed, God is but One God. If they do not desist from what they say, the disbelievers among them will be met with a painful chastisement' (5:73)*

وَقَالَتِ الْيَهُودُ يَدُ اللَّهِ مَغْلُولَةٌ ۚ غُلَّتْ أَيْدِيهِمْ وَلُعِنُوا بِمَا قَالُوا ۘ بَلْ يَدَاهُ
مَبْسُوطَتَانِ يُنْفِقُ كَيْفَ يَشَاءُ ۚ

> *"The Jews have said: 'God's hand is limited in what it can do. Limited are their hands, and they are cursed for what they have said. Indeed, His hands are open; he expends how He wills." (5:64)*

وَقَالَتِ الْيَهُودُ وَالنَّصَارَىٰ نَحْنُ أَبْنَاءُ اللَّهِ وَأَحِبَّاؤُهُ ۚ قُلْ فَلِمَ يُعَذِّبُكُمْ
بِذُنُوبِكُمْ ۖ بَلْ أَنْتُمْ بَشَرٌ مِمَّنْ خَلَقَ ۚ

> *"The Jews and Christians say: 'We are God's children and His favorites.' Say: 'Why then does He punish you for your offences? In fact, you are people just like others." (5:18)*

These societies are *jahili* also because their forms of worship, their customs and manners are derived from their false and distorted beliefs. They are also *jahili* societies because their institutions and their laws are not based on submission to

God alone. They neither accept the rule of God nor do they consider God's commandments as the only valid basis of all laws; on the contrary, they have established assemblies of men which have absolute power to legislate laws, thus usurping the right which belongs to God alone. At the time of Revelation, the Qur'an classified them among those who associate others with God, as they had given their priests and rabbis the authority to devise laws in whatever way they pleased.

اِتَّخَذُوْٓا اَحْبَارَهُمْ وَرُهْبَانَهُمْ اَرْبَابًا مِّنْ دُوْنِ اللّٰهِ وَالْمَسِيْحَ ابْنَ مَرْيَمَ ۚ وَمَآ
اُمِرُوْٓا اِلَّا لِيَعْبُدُوْٓا اِلٰهًا وَّاحِدًا ۚ لَآ اِلٰهَ اِلَّا هُوَ ؕ سُبْحٰنَهٗ عَمَّا يُشْرِكُوْنَ ﴿٣١﴾

***"They have taken their rabbis and priests as lords other than God, and the Messiah, son of Mary; and they were commanded to worship none but One God.. There is no god but He, glory be to Him above what they associate with Him!" (9:31)***

These people did not consider their priests or rabbis as divine, nor did they worship them; but they gave them the authority to make laws, obeying laws which were made by them not permitted by God. If at that time the Qur'an called them associaters of others with God and rejectors of truth, then today they are also the same, because today this authority is not in the hands of priests and rabbis but in the hands of individuals chosen from among themselves.

Lastly, all the existing .so — called 'Muslim' societies are also *jahili* societies.

We classify them among *jahili* societies not because they believe in other deities besides God or because they worship anyone other than God, but because their way of life is not based on submission to God alone. Although they believe in the Unity of God, still they have relegated the legislative attribute of God to others and submit to this authority, and from this authority they derive their systems, their traditions and customs, their laws, their values and standards, and almost every practice of life. God Most High says concerning rulers:

وَمَنْ لَّمْ يَحْكُمْ بِمَآ اَنْزَلَ اللّٰهُ فَاُولٰٓئِكَ هُمُ الْكٰفِرُوْنَ ﴿٤٤﴾

***"Those who do not judge according to what God has revealed are unbelievers." and concerning the ruled: (5:44)***

اَلَمْ تَرَ اِلَى الَّذِيْنَ يَزْعُمُوْنَ اَنَّهُمْ اٰمَنُوْا بِمَآ اُنْزِلَ اِلَيْكَ وَمَآ اُنْزِلَ مِنْ قَبْلِكَ
يُرِيْدُوْنَ اَنْ يَّتَحَاكَمُوْٓا اِلَى الطَّاغُوْتِ وَقَدْ اُمِرُوْٓا اَنْ يَّكْفُرُوْا بِهٖ ؕ

*"Have you not seen those who assert that they believe in what has been sent down to you and what was sent down before you, desiring to take their disputes to idols, while you were commanded to reject them?"* *(4:60)*

فَلَا وَرَبِّكَ لَا يُؤْمِنُونَ حَتَّىٰ يُحَكِّمُوكَ فِيمَا شَجَرَ بَيْنَهُمْ ثُمَّ لَا يَجِدُوا فِي أَنفُسِهِمْ حَرَجًا مِّمَّا قَضَيْتَ وَيُسَلِّمُوا تَسْلِيمًا ﴿٦٥﴾

***"But no, by your Lord, they have not believed until they make you judge regarding their disputes, and then do not find any resentment in their hearts against your verdict, but submit in full submission." (4:65)***

Before this, God accused the Jews and Christians of committing **Shirk**, (association of other gods with God) and of unbelief, and of taking priests and rabbis as lords in addition to God, only because they had given certain rights and privileges to their priests and rabbis, which today those who call themselves 'Muslims' have given to some people among themselves. This action of the Jews and Christians was considered by God in the same category of **Shirk** as that of the Christians' making Jesus into the Son of God and worshipping him. The latter is a rebellion against the Oneness of God, while the former is a rebellion against His prescribed way of life and a denial of "There is no other diety except God".

Among Muslim societies, some openly declare their 'secularism' and negate all their relationships with the religion; some others pay respect to the religion only with their mouths, but in their social life they have completely abandoned it. They say that they do not believe in the 'Unseen' and want to construct their social system on the basis of 'science', as science and the Unseen are contradictory! This claim of theirs is mere ignorance, and only ignorant people can talk like this.[17] There are some other societies which have given the authority of legislation to others besides God; they make whatever laws they please and then say, "This is the **Shari'ah** of God".

All these societies are the same in one respect, that none of them is based on submission to God alone. After explaining these facts, the position of Islam in relation to all these *jahili* societies can be described in one sentence: it considers all these societies unIslamic and illegal.

---

17 Refer to the discussion in Volume 7 of **Fi-Thilal** in explanation of the verse: "He has the keys to the Unseen; no one knows it except Him".

Islam does not look at the labels or titles which these societies have adopted; they all have one thing in common, and that is that their way of life is not based on complete submission to God alone. In this respect they share the same characteristic with a polytheistic society, the characteristic of ***Jahiliyyah***.

* * *

We have now come to the last of the points mentioned in the beginning of this chapter, and that point concerns the method which Islam adopts — today, tomorrow or in the remote future — in confronting actual human conditions. This method has been described in our discussion on the nature of the Muslim society, which is, in summary, that a Muslim society bases all its decisions on submission to God alone.

After defining this nature, we can immediately answer the following question: What is the principle on which human life ought to be based: — God's religion and its system of life, or some man — made system?

Islam answers this question in a clear cut and unambiguous manner: The only principle on which the totality of human life is to be based is God's religion and its system of life. If this principle is absent, the very first pillar of Islam — that is, bearing witness to — "**La ilaha illa Allah, Muhammadar Rasul Allah**" — will not be established nor its real influence felt. Unless this principle is accepted without any question and followed faithfully, the complete submission to God as taught by the Messenger of God — peace be on him — cannot be fulfilled.

وَمَآ اٰتٰىكُمُ الرَّسُوْلُ فَخُذُوْهُ وَمَا نَهٰىكُمْ عَنْهُ فَانْتَهُوْا

***"Whatever the Messenger gives you, accept it; whatever he, forbids you, refrain from it." (59:7)***

Furthermore, Islam asks: "Do you know better, or does God?" and then answers it: "God knows and, you do not know", and "You have been given only a little of the (true) knowledge".

The One Who knows, Who has created man, and Who is his Sustainer must be the Ruler, and His religion ought to be the way of life, and man should return to Him for guidance. As far as man — made theories and religions are concerned, they become outmoded and distorted, as they are based on the knowledge of men — those who do not know, and to whom only a little of the true knowledge is given.

God's religion is not a maze nor is its way of life a fluid thing, as the second part of the declaration of faith, "Muhammad is the Messenger of

God", clearly limits it. It is bounded by those principles which have come from the Messenger of God — peace be on him. If there is a clear text available from the Qur'an or from him, then that will be decisive and there will be no room for **Ijtihad** (using one's judgement). If no such clear judgement is available, then the time comes for **Ijtihad** — and that according to well — defined principles which are consistent with God's religion and not merely following opinions or desires.

يَاَيُّهَا الَّذِيْنَ اٰمَنُوْٓا اَطِيْعُوا اللّٰهَ وَ اَطِيْعُوا الرَّسُوْلَ وَ اُولِي الْاَمْرِ مِنْكُمْ ۚ فَاِنْ
تَنَازَعْتُمْ فِيْ شَيْءٍ فَرُدُّوْهُ اِلَى اللّٰهِ وَالرَّسُوْلِ

***"If you have difference of opinion concerning something, refer to God and His Messenger."***

*(4:59)*

The principles of **Ijtihad** and deduction are well known, and there is no vagueness or looseness in them. No one is allowed to devise a law and say that it is according to the Law of God unless it is declared that God is the Legislator, and that the source of authority is God Himself and not some nation or party or individual, and a sincere attempt is made to find out the will of God through reference to His Book and the teachings of His Messenger — peace be on him. But this right cannot be delegated to a person or persons who want to establish authority by taking the name of God, as was the case in Europe under the guise of 'the Church'. There is no 'Church' in Islam; no one can speak in the name of God except His Messenger — peace be on him. There are clear injunctions which define the limits of the Divine Law, the **Shari'ah**.

**"Al-din lil-waq'i"** ("the religion is for living") is a statement which is quite misunderstood and which is being used in a wrong sense. Certainly this religion is for living, but for what kind of life? This religion is for a life which is based on its principles, which is developed according to its methods. This life is completely harmonious with human nature and satisfies all human needs, needs which are determined only by the One Who creates and Who knows His creatures:

اَلَا يَعْلَمُ مَنْ خَلَقَ ؕ وَهُوَ اللَّطِيْفُ الْخَبِيْرُ ﴿۱۴﴾

***"Does He Who created not know His creatures? He is the All-Subtle, the All-Aware."*** *(67:14)*

It is not the function of religion to provide justification for whatever kind of life someone is leading and to bring an authority which he can use to justify his actions. Religion is to be a criterion, to approve what is good and to discard what is evil. If the whole system of life is against the religion, then its function is to abolish this system and to construct a new one. This is the meaning, according to Islam, of the saying "religion is for living"; one' ought to understand this with its correct meaning.

The question may be asked, "Is not the good of mankind the criterion for solving actual problems?" But again we will raise the question which Islam raises itself, and which it answers; that is, "Do you know better, or God?" and, "God knows, and you do not know."

The good of mankind is inherent in the Divine Laws sent down by God to the Prophet — peace be on him — which have come to us through his life. If at any time men think that their good is in going against what God has legislated, then first of all, they are deluded in their thinking.

إِنْ يَتَّبِعُونَ إِلَّا الظَّنَّ وَمَا تَهْوَى الْأَنْفُسُ ۖ وَلَقَدْ جَاءَهُمْ مِنْ رَبِّهِمُ الْهُدَىٰ ﴿٢٣﴾
أَمْ لِلْإِنْسَانِ مَا تَمَنَّىٰ ﴿٢٤﴾ فَلِلَّهِ الْآخِرَةُ وَالْأُولَىٰ ﴿٢٥﴾

> ***"they follow but speculation and their own desires, although guidance has come to them from their Sustainer. Or shall man have whatever he fancies? And to God belongs the first and the last."*** *(53: 23-25)*

Second, they are unbelievers. It is not possible for a person to declare that in his opinion good lies in going against what God has legislated, and simultaneously be a follower of this religion, or be considered its scholar, even for a single moment.

## *CHAPTER 6*

# THE UNIVERSAL LAW

Islam constructs its foundation of belief and action on the principle of total submission to God alone. Its beliefs, forms of worship and rules of life are uniformly an expression of this submission and are a practical interpretation of the declaration that there is no deity except God. The details of life are derived from the practice of the Messenger of God — peace be on him — and are a practical consequence of the declaration that Muhammad is the Messenger of God.

Islam builds its entire structure in such a way that these two parts of the declaration determine its system and its characteristics. When Islam builds its structure in this manner, giving it a separate and unique position among all other systems known to man, then Islam actually becomes harmonious with the universal law, which is operative not only in human existence but throughout the whole universe as well.

According to the Islamic concept, the whole universe has been created by God. The universe came into existence when God willed it and then He ordained certain natural laws which it follows and according to which all its various ,parts operate harmoniously:

إِنَّمَا قَوْلُنَا لِشَيْءٍ إِذَا أَرَدْنَاهُ أَن نَّقُولَ لَهُ كُن فَيَكُونُ ۝

***"When We wish to bring something into existence, We say to it, 'Be', and there it is."*** ***(16:40)***

الَّذِي لَهُ مُلْكُ السَّمَاوَاتِ وَالْأَرْضِ وَلَمْ يَتَّخِذْ
وَلَدًا وَلَمْ يَكُن لَّهُ شَرِيكٌ فِي الْمُلْكِ

***"And He created everything, and measured it in due proportion."*** ***(25:2)***

Behind this universe there is a Will which administers it, a Power which moves it, a Law which regulates it. This Power keeps a balance between the various parts of the universe and controls their motions; thus they neither collide with each other nor is there any disturbance in their system, nor do their regular motions come to a sudden stop; nor do they become disorganized. This will continue as long as the Divine will wishes it to continue. The whole universe is obedient to God's Will, His Power and His Authority; it is not possible for it to disobey the Divine Wili and its ordained law for a single moment. Due to this obedience and submission, the universe continues to go on in a harmonious fashion, and no destruction or dispersion or disturbance can enter into it unless God wills it.

إِنَّ رَبَّكُمُ اللَّهُ الَّذِي خَلَقَ السَّمَٰوَٰتِ وَالْأَرْضَ فِي سِتَّةِ أَيَّامٍ ثُمَّ اسْتَوَىٰ عَلَى
الْعَرْشِ يُغْشِي الَّيْلَ النَّهَارَ يَطْلُبُهُ حَثِيثًا وَالشَّمْسَ وَالْقَمَرَ وَالنُّجُومَ
مُسَخَّرَٰتٍ بِأَمْرِهِ أَلَا لَهُ الْخَلْقُ وَالْأَمْرُ تَبَارَكَ اللَّهُ رَبُّ الْعَٰلَمِينَ ۝

***"Indeed, your Sustainer is God, Who created the heavens and the earth in six periods and then established Himself upon the throne of sovereignty. He causes the night to cover up the day and the day to follow the night. The sun and the moon and the stars are controlled by His command, The creation and the command are for Him alone. Glorious is God, the Sustainer of the worlds."*** *(7:54)*

* * *

Man is a part of the universe; the laws which govern human nature are no different from the laws governing the universe. God is the Creator of the universe as well as of man. Man's body is made of earthly material, yet God has bestowed upon him certain characteristics which make him more than the earth from which he is made; God provides him according to a measure. In his bodily functions man involuntarily follows the same laws of nature as other creatures. His creation is according to the will of God rather than of his father and mother. The father and mother are able to come together; yet they are not able to transform a sperm into a human being. Man is born according to the method of development and the method of birth which God has prescribed for him; he breathes God's air in the quantity and fashion prescribed by God; he has feelings and understanding, he experiences pain, becomes hungry and thirsty, eats and drinks — in short, he has to live according to the laws of God and he has no choice in the matter. In this respect there is no difference between him and other inanimate or animate objects of the universe. All unconditionally submit to the Will of God and to the laws of His creation.

He Who has created the universe and man, and Who made man obedient to the laws which also govern the universe, has also prescribed a **Shari'ah** for his voluntary actions. If man follows this law, then his life is in harmony with his own nature. From this point of view, this **Shari'ah** is also a part of that universal law which governs the entire universe, including the physical and biological aspects of man.

Each word of God, whether it is an injunction or a prohibition, a promise or an admonition, a rule or guidance, is a part of the universal law and is as accurate and true as any of the laws known as the "laws of nature" — the Divinely ordained laws for the universe — which we find to be operative every moment according to what God has prescribed for them from the dawn of creation.

Thus the **Shari'ah** which God has given to man to organize his life is also a universal law, as it is related to the general law of the universe and is harmonious with it. This obedience to the **Shari'ah** becomes a necessity for human beings so that their lives may become harmonious and in tune with the rest of the universe; not only this, but the only way in which harmony can be brought about between the physical laws which are operative in the biological life of a man and the moral laws which govern his voluntary actions is solely through obedience to the **Shari'ah**. Only in this way does man's personality, internal and external, become integrated.

Man cannot understand all the laws of the universe, nor can he comprehend the unity of this system; he cannot even understand the laws which govern his own person, from which he cannot deviate by a hair's breadth. Thus he is incapable of making laws for a system of life which can be in complete harmony with the universe or which can even harmonize his physical needs with his external behaviour. This capability belongs solely to the Creator of the universe and of men, Who not only controls the universe but also human affairs, and Who implements a uniform law according to His will.

This obedience to the **Shari'ah** of God is necessary for the sake of this harmony, even more necessary than the establishment of the Islamic beief, as no individual or group of individuals can be truly Muslim until they wholly submit to God alone in the manner taught by the Messenger of God — peace be on him, thus testifying by their actions that there is no deity except God and that Muhammad is God's Messenger.

Total harmony between human life and the law of the universe is entirely beneficial for mankind, as this is the only guarantee against any kind of discord in life. Only in this state will they be at peace with themselves and at peace with the universe, living in accord with its laws and its movements. In the same way, they will have peace of mind, as their actions will agree with their true natural demands, with no conflict between the two. Indeed, the Shari'ah of God harmonizes the external behaviour of man with his internal nature in an easy way. When a man makes peace with his own nature, peace and cooperation among individuals follow automatically, as they all live together under one system, which is a part of the general system of the universe.

Thus, blessings fall on all mankind, as this way leads in an easy manner to the knowledge of the secrets of nature, its hidden, forces, and the treasures concealed in the expanses of the universe. Man uses these for the benefit of all mankind, under the guidance of the Shari'ah of God, without any conflict or competition.

وَلَوِ اتَّبَعَ الْحَقُّ أَهْوَاءَهُمْ لَفَسَدَتِ السَّمَاوَاتُ وَالْأَرْضُ وَمَن فِيهِنَّ ۚ بَلْ
أَتَيْنَاهُم بِذِكْرِهِمْ فَهُمْ عَن ذِكْرِهِم مُّعْرِضُونَ ﴿٧١﴾

***In contrast to the Shari'ah of God are men's whims: "Had the truth followed their opinions, the heavens and the earth and whosoever is in them would surely have been corrupted."*** *(23:71)*

From this we come to know that the truth is one and not many. It is the foundation of this religion, the heavens and earth are based upon it, all the affairs of this world and of the next are settled by it, man will be accountable to God on the basis of it, and those who deviate from the truth are punished by it, and people will be judged by God according to it. Truth is indivisible, and it is the name of that general law which God has ordained for all affairs; and everything in existence either follows it or is punished by it.

لَقَدْ أَنزَلْنَا إِلَيْكُمْ كِتَابًا فِيهِ ذِكْرُكُمْ ۖ أَفَلَا تَعْقِلُونَ ﴿١٠﴾ وَكَمْ قَصَمْنَا مِن قَرْيَةٍ
كَانَتْ ظَالِمَةً وَأَنشَأْنَا بَعْدَهَا قَوْمًا آخَرِينَ ﴿١١﴾ فَلَمَّا أَحَسُّوا بَأْسَنَا إِذَا هُم
مِّنْهَا يَرْكُضُونَ ﴿١٢﴾ لَا تَرْكُضُوا وَارْجِعُوا إِلَىٰ مَا أُتْرِفْتُمْ فِيهِ وَمَسَاكِنِكُمْ لَعَلَّكُمْ
تُسْأَلُونَ ﴿١٣﴾ قَالُوا يَا وَيْلَنَا إِنَّا كُنَّا ظَالِمِينَ ﴿١٤﴾ فَمَا زَالَت تِّلْكَ دَعْوَاهُمْ حَتَّىٰ
جَعَلْنَاهُمْ حَصِيدًا خَامِدِينَ ﴿١٥﴾ وَمَا خَلَقْنَا السَّمَاءَ وَالْأَرْضَ وَمَا بَيْنَهُمَا لَاعِبِينَ ﴿١٦﴾
لَوْ أَرَدْنَا أَن نَّتَّخِذَ لَهْوًا لَّاتَّخَذْنَاهُ مِن لَّدُنَّا إِن كُنَّا فَاعِلِينَ ﴿١٧﴾ بَلْ نَقْذِفُ

بِالْحَقِّ عَلَى الْبَاطِلِ فَيَدْمَغُهُ فَإِذَا هُوَ زَاهِقٌ ۚ وَلَكُمُ الْوَيْلُ مِمَّا تَصِفُونَ ﴿١٨﴾ وَلَهُ
مَنْ فِي السَّمَاوَاتِ وَالْأَرْضِ ۚ وَمَنْ عِنْدَهُ لَا يَسْتَكْبِرُونَ عَنْ عِبَادَتِهِ وَلَا
يَسْتَحْسِرُونَ ﴿١٩﴾ يُسَبِّحُونَ اللَّيْلَ وَالنَّهَارَ لَا يَفْتُرُونَ ﴿٢٠﴾

*"We have sent to you a Book which speaks about you; do you not then use your reason? Many a wicked town have We destroyed and have replaced them with other people. When they felt Our Might approaching, they started to run. (It was said to them), 'Do not run; return to the luxury that you gloated in and to your homes; maybe you shall be questioned'.*

*They said: 'Woe upon us! We have been evil — doers'. So they did not stop crying until We made them stubble, silent and still. We did not create the heavens and the earth and whatsoever is between them as a sport. Had We desired to adopt it for Us as a diversion, We would have taken it to Us from Ourselves, had We done so. Nay, but We held the truth against falsehood, and it prevails over it, and behold! falsehood vanishes away. Then woe to you for what you ascribe (to God). To Him belongs whatsoever is in the heavens and the earth, and those who are with Him do not be — come too proud ,to worship Him; neither do they grow weary of glorifying Him by night and by day and never failing."*

*(21: 10-20)*

Human nature in its depths has full awareness of this truth. Man's form and body, and the organization of the vast universe around him, reminds him that this universe is based on truth, and truth is its essence, and it is related to a central law which sustains it. Thus, there is no disturbance in it, no conflict between its parts; it does not move at random, nor does it depend on chance, nor is it devoid of an overall plan; neither is it a sport in the hands of human caprices, but runs smoothly on a precise, detailed and prescribed course. Conflict begins when man deviates from the truth which is hidden in the depths of his own nature, under the influence of his desires, and when he follows laws based on his own opinions instead of following God's commandments. Instead of submitting to his True Master along with the rest of the universe, he rebels and revolts.

When this conflict between man and his own nature, and man and the universe, spreads to human groups, nations and races, then all the forces and resources of the universe are utilized not for the benefit of all mankind, but for its destruction and for violence against others.

It becomes clear from the above discussion that the purpose of the establishment of God's law on earth is not merely for the sake of the next world. This world and the next world are not two separate entities, but are stages complementary to each other. The law given by God not only harmonizes these two stages but also harmonizes human life with the general law of the universe. Thus, when harmony between human life and the universe ensues, its results are not postponed for the next world but are operative even in this world. However, they will reach their perfection in the Hereafter.

* * *

This, then, is the foundation of the Islamic concept of the universe and of human life as a part of this universe. By its very nature, this concept is different from all other concepts known to mankind. This is why this concept implies certain responsibilities and obligations which are not found in other concepts of life.

According to this concept, obedience to the **Shari'ah** of God is actually a consequence of the need to harmonize human life with that law which is operative within man himself and in the rest of the universe. This need demands that the law which governs the social affairs of human beings should be in accordance with the general law of the universe; it demands that man submit to God alone, with the rest of the universe, and that no man should claim lordship over others. A suggestion of this need for harmony which we have been talking about is found in the conversation between Abraham — peace be on him — the father of the Muslim community, and Nimrod. This man was a tyrant and claimed absolute sovereignty over his subjects; yet he did not claim sovereignty over the heavens, the planets and stars. When the Prophet Abraham — peace be on him — put forward the argument that He Who has authority over the universe is the only One to have authority over human beings too, he became speechless:

أَلَمْ تَرَ إِلَى الَّذِي حَاجَّ إِبْرَاهِيمَ فِي رَبِّهِ أَنْ آتَاهُ اللَّهُ الْمُلْكَ إِذْ قَالَ إِبْرَاهِيمُ رَبِّيَ الَّذِي
يُحْيِي وَيُمِيتُ قَالَ أَنَا أُحْيِي وَأُمِيتُ قَالَ إِبْرَاهِيمُ فَإِنَّ اللَّهَ يَأْتِي بِالشَّمْسِ مِنَ الْمَشْرِقِ
فَأْتِ بِهَا مِنَ الْمَغْرِبِ فَبُهِتَ الَّذِي كَفَرَ وَاللَّهُ لَا يَهْدِي الْقَوْمَ الظَّالِمِينَ ﴿٢٥٨﴾

*"Have you considered the case of the man who argued with Abraham concerning his Sustainer, because God had given him rule over a country? When Abraham said: My Lord is He Who gives life and Who gives death,' he replied: 'I give life and I give death.' Abraham said: 'Indeed, God brings out the sun from the east. Then do you bring it out from the west?' Then the unbeliever became speechless. And God does not guide the evil — doing people".* *(2: 258)*

أَفَغَيْرَ دِينِ اللّٰهِ يَبْغُونَ وَلَهُ أَسْلَمَ مَنْ فِي السَّمٰوٰتِ وَالْأَرْضِ طَوْعًا
وَّكَرْهًا وَّإِلَيْهِ يُرْجَعُونَ ﴿٨٣﴾

*"Do they seek a religion other than the religion of God, while whatever is in the heavens and the earth submits to Him willingly, and will return to Him?"* *(3:83)*

## *CHAPTER 7*

# ISLAM IS THE REAL CIVILIZATION

Islam knows only two kinds of societies, the Islamic and the *jahili*. The islamic society is that which follows Islam in belief and ways of worship, in law and organization, in morals and manners. The *jahili* society is that which does not follow Islam and in which neither the Islamic belief and concepts, nor Islamic values or standards, Islamic laws and regulations, or Islamic morals and manners are cared for.

The Islamic society is not one in which people call themselves 'Muslims' but in which the Islamic law has no status, even though prayer, fasting and Hajj are regularly observed; and the Islamic society is not one in which people invent their own version of Islam, other than what God and His Messenger — peace be on him — have prescribed and explained, and call it, for example, 'progressive Islam'.

***Jahili*** society appears in various forms, all of them ignorant of the Divine guidance.

Sometimes it takes the form of a society in which belief in God is denied and human history is explained in terms of intellectual materialism, and 'scientific socialism' becomes its system.

Sometimes it appears in the form of a society in which God's existence is not denied, but His domain is restricted to the heavens and His rule on earth is suspended. Neither the **Shari'ah** nor the values prescribed by God and ordained by Him as eternal and invariable find any place in this scheme of life. In this society, people are permitted to go to mosques, churches and synagogues; yet it does not tolerate people's demanding that the **Shari'ah** of God be applied in their daily affairs. Thus, such a society denies or suspends God's soverignty on earth, while God says plainly:

وَهُوَ الَّذِي فِي السَّمَاءِ إِلَٰهٌ وَفِي الْأَرْضِ إِلَٰهٌ

***"It is He Who is Sovereign in the heavens and***

> ***Sovereign in the earth."*** *(46:84)*

Because of this behaviour, such a society does not follow the religion of God as defined by Him:

> إِنِ الْحُكْمُ إِلَّا لِلَّهِ ۚ أَمَرَ أَلَّا تَعْبُدُوا إِلَّا إِيَّاهُ ۚ ذَٰلِكَ الدِّينُ الْقَيِّمُ
>
> ***"The command belongs to God alone. He commands you not to worship anyone except Him. This is the right way of life."*** *(12:40)*

Because of this, such a society is to be counted among ***jahili*** societies, although it may proclaim belief in God and permit people to observe their devotions in mosques, churches and synagogues.

The Islamic society is, by its very nature, the only civilized society, and the ***jahili*** societies, in all their various forms, are backward societies. It is necessary to elucidate this great truth.

Once I announced as the title of a book of mine which was in press, **The Civilized Society of Islam;** but in my next announcement I dropped the word 'civilized' from it. At this change, an Algerian author (who writes in French) commented that the reason for this change is that psychology which operates in a person's mind while defending Islam. The author expressed regret that this was an expression of immaturity which was preventing me from facing reality!

I excused this Algerian author because at one time I myself was of the same opinion. At that time, my thought processes were similar to his thought processes of today. I encountered the same difficulty which he is encountering today; that is, to understand the meaning of 'civilization'.

Until then, I had not gotten rid of the cultural influences which had penetrated my mind in spite of my Islamic attitude and inclination. The source of these influences was foreign — alien to my Islamic consciousness, — yet these influences had clouded by intuition and concepts. The Western concept of civilization was my standard; it had prevented me from seeing with clear and penetrating vision.

However, later I saw very clearly that the Muslim society was the civilized society. Hence the word 'civilized' in the title of my book was redundant and did not add anything new; rather it would have obscured the thinking of the reader in the same way as my own ideas had been obscured.

Now the question is, what is the meaning of 'civilization?' Let us try to explain it.

When, in a society, the sovereignty belongs to God alone, expressed in its obedience to the Divine Law, only then is every person in that society free from servitude to others, and only then does he taste true freedom. This alone is 'human civilization', as the basis of a human civilization is the complete and true freedom of every person and the full dignity of every individual of the society. On the other hand, in a society in which some people are lords who legislate and some others are slaves who obey them, then there is no freedom in the real sense, nor dignity for each and every individual.

It is necessary that we clarify the point that legislation is not limited only to legal matters, as some people assign this narrow meaning to the **Shari'ah**. The fact is that attitudes, the way of living, the values, criteria, habits and traditions, are all legislated and affect people. If a particular group of people forges all these chains and imprisons others in them, this will not be a free society. In such a society some people have the position of authority, while others are subservient to them; hence this society will be backward, and in Islamic terminology is called a '*jahili*' society.

Only Islamic society is unique in this respect, in that the authority belongs to God alone; and man, cutting off his chains of servitude to other human beings, enters into the service of God and thus attains that real and complete freedom which is the focus of human civilization. In this society, the dignity and honor of man are respected according to what God has prescribed. He becomes the representative of God on earth, and his position becomes even higher than that of the angels.

* * *

In a society which bases its foundation on the concept, belief and way of life which all originate from the One God, man's dignity is respected to the highest degree and no one is a slave to another, as they are in societies in which the concepts, beliefs and way of life originate from human masters. In the former society, man's highest characteristics — those of the spirit and mind — are reflected, while in a society in which human relationships are based on color, race or nation, or similar criteria, these relationships become a chain for human thought and prevent man's noble characteristics from coming to the fore. A person remains human regardless of what color, race or nation he belongs to, but he cannot be called human if he is devoid of spirit and reason. Furthermore, he is able to change his beliefs, concepts and attitudes toward life, but he is incapable of changing his color and race, nor can he decide in what place or nation to be born. Thus it is clear that only such a society is civilized in which human associations are based on free choice, and that society is backward in which the basis of association is something other than free choice; in Islamic terminology, it is a '*jahili* society'.

Only Islam has the distinction of basing the fundamental binding relationship in its society on belief; and on the basis of this belief, black and white and red and yellow, Arabs and Greeks, Persians and Africans, and all nations which inhabit the earth become one community. In this society God is the Lord and only He is worshipped, the most honorable is the one who is noblest in character, and all individuals are equally subject to a law which is not man — made but made by their Creator.

* * *

A society which places the highest value on the 'humanity' of man and honours the noble 'human' characteristics is truly civilized. If materialism, no matter in what form, is given the highest value, whether it be in the form of a 'theory', such as in the Marxist interpretation of history, or in the form of material production, as is the case with the United States and European countries, and all other human values are sacrificed at its altar, then such a society is a backward one, or, in Islamic terminology, is a '*jahili* society'.

The civilized society — that is, the Islamic society — does not downgrade matter, either in theory or in the form of material production, as it considers the universe in which we live, by which we are influenced, and which we influence, to be made of matter, and it considers material production to be the backbone of the vice — gerency of God on earth. However, in the Islamic society material comforts are not made into the highest value at the expense of 'human' characteristics — freedom and honor, family and its obligations, morals and values, and so on — as is the case in *jahili* societies.

If a society . is based on 'human values' and 'human morals' and these remain dominant in it, then that society will be civilized. Human values and human morals are not something mysterious and undefinable, nor are they 'progressive' and changeable, having no roots and stability, as is claimed by the exponents of the materialistic interpretation of history or of 'scientific socialism.' They are the values and the morals which develop those characteristics in a human being which distinguish him from the animals and which emphasize those aspects of his personality which raise him above the animals; these are not such values and morals which develop and emphasize those characteristics in man which are common with the animals.

When the question is viewed in this manner, a fixed and well — defined line of separation is obtained which cannot be erased by the incessant attempt of the 'progressives' and the scientific societies to erase it. According to this view, moral standards are not determined by the environment and changing conditions; rather they are fixed criteria above and beyond the difference in environments. One cannot say that some moral values are 'agricultural' and others 'industrial', some are 'capitalistic' and some others 'socialistic', some are 'bourgeoise' and others 'proletarian'. Here, the standards of morality are independent of the environment, the economic status, and the stage of development of a society; these are nothing but superficial variations. Beyond all these, we arrive at 'human' values and morals and at 'animalistic' values and morals, this being the correct separation or, in Islamic terminology, 'Islamic values and morals and '***jahili***' values and morals.

Indeed, Islam establishes the values and morals which are 'human' — those which develop characteristics in a human being which distinguish him from the animals. In whatever society Islam is dominant, whether it is an agricultural or industrial society, nomadic and pastoral or urban and settled, poor or rich, it implants these human values and morals, nurtures them and strengthens them; it develops human characteristics progressively and guards against degeneration toward animalism. The direction of the line which separates human values from animal-like characteristics is upward; but if this direction is reversed, then in spite of all material progress the civilization will be 'backward', 'degenerative', and '***jahili***'!

* * *

If the family is the basis of the society, and the basis of the family is the division of labour between husband and wife, and the upbringing of children is the most important function of the family, then such a society is indeed civilized. In the Islamic system of life, this kind of a family provides the environment under which human values and morals develop and grow in the new generation; these values and morals cannot exist apart from the family unit. If, on the other hand, free sexual relationships and illegitimate children become the basis of a society, and if the relationship between man and woman is based on lust, passion and impulse, and the division of work is not based on family responsibility and natural gifts; if woman's role is merely to be attractive, sexy and flirtatious, and if woman is freed from her basic responsibility of bringing up children; and if, on her own or under social demand, she prefers to become a hostess or a stewardess in a hotel or ship or air company, thus spending her ability for material productivity rather than in the training of human beings, because material production is considered to be more important, more valuable and more honourable than the development of human character, then such a civilization is 'backward' from the human point of view, or in the Islamic terminology.

The family system and the relationship between the sexes determine the whole character of a society and whether it is backward or civilized, ***jahili*** or Islamic. Those societies which give ascendance to physical desires and animalistic morals cannot be considered civilized, no matter how much progress they may make in industry or science. This is the only measure which does not err in gauging true human progress.

In all modern ***jahili*** societies, the meaning of 'morality' is limited to such an extent that all those aspects which distinguish man from animal are considered beyond its sphere. In these societies, illegitimate sexual relationships, even homosexuality, are not considered immoral. The meaning of ethics is limited to economic affairs or sometimes to political affairs which fall into the category of 'government interests'. For example, the scandal of Christine. Keeler and the British minister Profumo was not considered serious to British society because of its sexual aspect; it was condemnable because Christine Keeler was also involved with a naval attache of the Russian Embassy, and thus her association with a cabinet minister lied before the British Parliament! Similar scandals come to light in the American Senate. Englishmen and Americans who get involved in such spying scandals usually take refuge in Russia. These affairs are not considered immoral because of sexual deviations, but because of the danger to state secrets!

Among ***jahili*** societies, writers, journalists and editors advise both married and unmarried people that free sexual relation ships are not immoral. However, it is immoral if a boy uses his partner, or a girl uses her partner, for sex, while feeling no love in his or her heart. It is bad if a wife continues to guard her chastity while hfr love for her husband has vanished; it is admirable if she finds another lover. Dozens of stories are written about this theme; many newspaper editorials, ankles, cartoons, serious and light columns all invite to this way of life.

From the point of view of 'human' progress, all such societies are not civilized but are backward.

The line of human progress goes upward from animal desires toward higher values. To control the animal desires, a progressive society lays down the foundation of a family system in which human desires find satisfaction, as well as providing for the future generation to be brought up in such a manner that it will continue the human civilization, in which human characteristics flower to their full bloom. Obviously a society which intends to control the animal characteristics, while providing full opportunities for the development and perfection of human characteristics, requires strong safeguards for the peace and stability of the family, so that it may perform its basic task free from the influences of impulsive passions. On the other hand, if in a society immoral teachings and poisonous suggestions are rampant, and sexual activity is considered outside the sphere of morality, then in that society the humanity of man can hardly find a place to develop.

Thus, only Islamic values and morals, Islamic teachings and safeguards, are worthy of mankind, and from this unchanging and true measure of human progress, Islam is the real civilization and Islamic society is truly civilized.

* * *

Lastly, when man establishes the representation of God on earth in all respects, by dedicating himself to the service of God and freeing himself from servitude to others, by establishing the system of life prescribed by God and rejecting all other systems, by arranging his life according to the **Shari'ah** of God and giving up all other laws, by adopting the values and standards of morality which are pleasing to God and rejecting all other standards and, after this, when he investigates the laws governing the universe and uses them for the benefit of all mankind, applies them to resources hidden in the earth in accordance with the obligation imposed on him by God as His vicegerent on earth, unearths the treasures and resources of food and raw materials for industries, and uses his technical and professional knowledge for the development of various o kinds of industries, doing all these things as a God — fearing person and as a representative of God; and when his attitude toward the material and moral aspects of life is infused with this spirit, only then does man become completely civilized and the society reach the height of civilization. In Islam, mere material inventions are not considered as civilization, as a ***jahili*** society can also have material prosperity. In many places in the Qur'an, God has described societies of this kind, which have attained material prosperity while remaining ***jahili***.

أَتَبْنُونَ بِكُلِّ رِيعٍ آيَةً تَعْبَثُونَ ﴿١٢٨﴾ وَتَتَّخِذُونَ مَصَانِعَ لَعَلَّكُمْ تَخْلُدُونَ ﴿١٢٩﴾
وَإِذَا بَطَشْتُم بَطَشْتُمْ جَبَّارِينَ ﴿١٣٠﴾ فَاتَّقُوا اللَّهَ وَأَطِيعُونِ ﴿١٣١﴾ وَاتَّقُوا الَّذِي
أَمَدَّكُم بِمَا تَعْلَمُونَ ﴿١٣٢﴾ أَمَدَّكُم بِأَنْعَامٍ وَبَنِينَ ﴿١٣٣﴾ وَجَنَّاتٍ وَعُيُونٍ ﴿١٣٤﴾ إِنِّي
أَخَافُ عَلَيْكُمْ عَذَابَ يَوْمٍ عَظِيمٍ ﴿١٣٥﴾

***(Hud said to his people): "What is the matter with you that you make a memorial at every high***

*place and build palaces as if you are immortal? When you deal with others, you are tyrants. Then fear God, and obey me. Fear Him Who gave you whatever you know. He gave you animals, children, gardens and rivers. I fear for you the day of a severe chastisement."* *(26:128-135)*

أَتُتْرَكُونَ فِي مَا هٰهُنَآ اٰمِنِينَ ﴿١٤٦﴾ فِي جَنّٰتٍ وَّعُيُونٍ ﴿١٤٧﴾ وَّزُرُوعٍ وَّنَخْلٍ طَلْعُهَا
هَضِيمٌ ﴿١٤٨﴾ وَتَنْحِتُونَ مِنَ الْجِبَالِ بُيُوتًا فٰرِهِينَ ﴿١٤٩﴾ فَاتَّقُوا اللّٰهَ وَاَطِيعُونِ ﴿١٥٠﴾
وَلَا تُطِيعُوٓا اَمْرَ الْمُسْرِفِينَ ﴿١٥١﴾ الَّذِينَ يُفْسِدُونَ فِي الْاَرْضِ وَلَا يُصْلِحُونَ ﴿١٥٢﴾

*(Salih said to his people): "Will you remain secure here among these things — among gardens and fountains, the farmland and palm trees with juicy fruit? You build houses skillfully out of the mountains. So fear God and obey me, and do not obey the advice of the wasteful, those who make corruption in the earth and do not set things right."* *(26:146-152)*

فَلَمَّا نَسُوا مَا ذُكِّرُوا بِهٖ فَتَحْنَا عَلَيْهِمْ اَبْوَابَ كُلِّ شَيْءٍ حَتّٰٓى اِذَا فَرِحُوا بِمَآ اُوتُوٓا
اَخَذْنٰهُمْ بَغْتَةً فَاِذَا هُمْ مُّبْلِسُونَ ﴿٤٤﴾ فَقُطِعَ دَابِرُ الْقَوْمِ الَّذِينَ ظَلَمُوا
وَالْحَمْدُ لِلّٰهِ رَبِّ الْعٰلَمِينَ ﴿٤٥﴾

*"So when they forgot what they were reminded of, We opened to them the gates of everything until, when they rejoiced in what they were given, We seized them suddenly, and behold! they were greatly confounded. So the last remnant of the people who did evil was cut off. Praise belongs to God, the Sustainer of the Worlds."* *(6: 44-45)*

اِنَّمَا مَثَلُ الْحَيٰوةِ الدُّنْيَا كَمَآءٍ اَنْزَلْنٰهُ مِنَ السَّمَآءِ فَاخْتَلَطَ بِهٖ نَبَاتُ الْاَرْضِ
مِمَّا يَاْكُلُ النَّاسُ وَالْاَنْعَامُ حَتّٰٓى اِذَآ اَخَذَتِ الْاَرْضُ زُخْرُفَهَا وَازَّيَّنَتْ
وَظَنَّ اَهْلُهَآ اَنَّهُمْ قٰدِرُونَ عَلَيْهَآ اَتٰهَآ اَمْرُنَا لَيْلًا اَوْ نَهَارًا فَجَعَلْنٰهَا
حَصِيدًا كَاَنْ لَّمْ تَغْنَ بِالْاَمْسِ

*"When the earth has taken on its glitter and has*

> ***adorned itself fair, and its inhabitants think they have power over it, Our command comes upon it by night or by day, and We make it as stubble, as if yesterday it had not flourished."*** *(10:24)*

But as we have said earlier, Islam does not look with contempt on material progress and material inventions; in fact, it considers them when used under the Divine system of life, as God's gifts. In the Qur'an we find that God promises His bounty to people when they are obedient to Him.

فَقُلْتُ اسْتَغْفِرُوا رَبَّكُمْ إِنَّهُ كَانَ غَفَّارًا ﴿١٠﴾ يُرْسِلِ السَّمَاءَ عَلَيْكُمْ مِدْرَارًا ﴿١١﴾
وَيُمْدِدْكُمْ بِأَمْوَالٍ وَبَنِينَ وَيَجْعَلْ لَكُمْ جَنَّاتٍ وَيَجْعَلْ لَكُمْ أَنْهَارًا ﴿١٢﴾

> ***(Noah said): "I said to my people, 'Ask forgiveness from your Sustainer; indeed, He accepts repentance. He will send upon you rain from the sky continuously and will make you powerful through wealth and children, and He will raise for you gardens and make streams for you."*** *(71:10-12)*

وَلَوْ أَنَّ أَهْلَ الْقُرَىٰ آمَنُوا وَاتَّقَوْا لَفَتَحْنَا عَلَيْهِمْ بَرَكَاتٍ مِنَ السَّمَاءِ وَالْأَرْضِ
وَلَٰكِنْ كَذَّبُوا فَأَخَذْنَاهُمْ بِمَا كَانُوا يَكْسِبُونَ ﴿٩٦﴾

> ***"Had the people of those towns believed and feared God, We would have opened blessings upon them from the sky and the earth, but they rejected the truth, so for their evil deeds We took them to account."*** *(7:96)*

But the important thing is that foundation on which the industrial structure is built, and those values which bind a society, and through which a society acquires the characteristics of the 'human civilization'.

* * *

Since the basis of the Islamic society and the nature of its growth, which give rise to its community, have a unique character, one cannot apply to it those theories which can explain the establishment and growth of *jahili* societies. The Islamic society is born out of a movement, and this movement continues within it; it determines the places and positions of individuals in the community and then assigns them roles and responsibilities.

The origin of this movement, from which this community is born, is outside the human sphere and outside this world. Its source is a belief which has come from God to mankind, and which gives them a particular concept of the universe, of life of human history, of values and purposes, and which defines for them a way of life reflecting this concept. Thus the initial impetus for the movement does not come from human minds, nor from the physical world, but, as we have stated before, it comes from outside the earth and outside the human sphere; and this is the first distinctive feature of the Islamic society and its organization. Indeed, the origin of this movement is an element outside the sphere of man and outside the physical world. This element, which comes into existence from God's will, is not something expected by any human being or taken into consideration by anyone, and in the beginning, no human endeavor enters into it. This Divine element sows the seed of the Islamic movement and at the same time prepares the human being for action —prepares the one who believes in the faith which reaches to him from the Divine source. As soon as this single individual believes in this — faith, the Islamic community comes into existence (potentially). This individual does not remain satisfied at having this faith, but stands up to give its message. It is the nature of this faith that it is a virile and dynamic movement; the power which lights up this faith in this heart knows that it will not remain concealed but will come out into the open and will spread to others.

When the number of Believers reaches three, then this faith tells them; "Now you are a community, a distinct Islamic community, distinct from that ***jahili*** society which does not live according to this belief or accept its basic premise." Now the Islamic society has come into existence (actually).

These three individuals increase to ten, the ten to a hundred, the hundred to a thousand, and the thousand increase to twelve thousand — and the Islamic society grows and becomes established.

During the progress of this movement, a struggle would already have started within the ***jahili*** society. On the one side is this new born society, which in its belief and concepts, values and standards, existence and organization has separated itself from the ***jahili*** society, from which the Islamic society absorbs individuals. This movement, from the moment of its inception until the growth and permanent existence of its society comes about, tests every individual and assigns him a position of responsibility according to his capacity, as measured by the Islamic balance and standards. The society automatically recognizes his capabilities, and he does not need to come forward and announce his candidacy; in fact, his belief and the values to which he and his society subscribe compel him to keep himself concealed from the eyes of those who want to give him a responsible position.

But the movement which is a natural outgrowth of the Islamic belief and which is the essence of the Islamic society does not let any individual hide himself. Every individual of this society must move! There should be a movement in his belief, a movement in his blood, a movement in his community, and in the structure of this organic society, and as the ***Jahiliyyah*** is all around him, and its residual influences in his mind and in the minds of those around him, the struggle goes on and the Jihaad continues until the Day of Resurrection.

The ups and downs through which the movement passes determine the position and activity of every individual in the movement, and the organic body of this society is completed through the harmony between its individuals and their activities.

This kind of beginning and this method of organization are two of the characteristics of the Islamic society which distinguish it from other societies in respect to its existence and its structure, its nature and its form, its system and the method of regulating this system, and 'make it a unique and separate entity. It cannot be understood by social theories alien to it, nor can it be taught by methods foreign to its nature, nor can it be brought into existence by ways borrowed from other systems.

* * *

According to our unvarying definition of civilization, the Islamic society is not just an entity of the past, to be studied in history, but it is a demand of the present and a hope of the future. Mankind can be dignified, today or tomorrow, by striving toward this noble civilization, by pulling itself out of the abyss of ***Jahiliyyah*** into which it is falling. This is true not only for the industrially and economically developed nations but also for the backward nations.

The values to which we referred above as human values were never attained by mankind except in the period of Islamic civilization. We also ought to remember that by the term 'Islamic Civilization' we mean that civilization in which these values are found to the highest degree, and not a civilization which may make progress in industry, economics and science but in which human values are suppressed.

These values are not idealistic but are practical values which can be attained through human effort, by applying the teachings of Islam correctly. These values can be attained in any environment, whatever the level of industrial and scientific progress may be, as there is no contradiction; in fact, material prosperity and scientific progress are encouraged by the teachings of Islam, as they pretain to man's role as the representative of God on earth.

Similarly, in countries which are industrially and scientifically backward, these values teach people not to remain just silent spectators but to strive for industrial and scientific progress. A civilization with these values can develop anywhere and in any environment; however, the actual form it takes is not one, but depends on the conditions and environment existing in the society in which these values develop.

The Islamic society, in its form and extent and its way of living, is not a fixed historic entity; but its existence and its civilization are based on values which are fixed historical realities. The word 'historical' used in this context only means that these values took concrete form in a particular period of human history. In fact, these values, by their nature, do not belong to any particular period; they are the truth which has come to man from the Divine source — beyond the sphere of mankind and beyond the sphere of the physical universe.

The Islamic civilization can take various forms in its material and organizational structure, but the principles and values on which it is based are eternal and unchangeable. These are: the worship of God alone, the foundation of human relationships on the belief in the Oneness of God, the supremacy of the humanity of man over material things, the development of human values and the control of animalistic desires, respect for the family, the assumption of being the representative of God on earth according to His guidance and instruction, and in all affairs of this vicegerency the rule of God's law (**al-Shari'ah**) and the way of life prescribed by Him.

The forms of the Islamic civilization, constructed on these fixed principles, depend on actual conditions and are influenced by and change according to the stage of industrial, economic or scientific progress. These forms are necessarily different and are a consequence of the fact that Islam possesses sufficient flexibility to enter into any system and mold that system according to its purposes; but this flexibility in the outward forms of Islamic civilization does not mean any flexibility in the Islamic belief, which is the fountainhead of this civilization, nor is it to be considered as borrowed from outside, for it is the character of this religion. However, flexibility is not to be confused with fluidity. There is a great difference between these two.

When Islam entered the central part of Africa, it clothed naked human beings, socialized them, brought them out of the deep recesses of isolation, and taught them the joy of work for exploring material resources. It brought them out of the narrow circles of tribe and clan into the vast circle of the Islamic community, and out of the worship of pagan gods into the worship of the Creator of the worlds. If this is not civilization, then what is it? This civilization was for this environment, and it used the actual resources which were available. If Islam enters into some other environment, then its civilization will also take another form — but with values which are eternal, — based on the existing resources of that particular environment.

Thus, the development of the civilization, according to the method and manner of Islam, does not depend on any particular level of industrial, economic or scientific progress. Wherever this civilization is established, it will use all the resources, will develop them, and if in a certain place these resources are non — existent, then it will supply them and will provide the means for their growth and progress. But in all situations it will be based on its immutable and eternal principles, and wherever such an Islamic society comes into existence, its particular character and its particular movement will also come into existence, and will make it distinguished and distinct from all *jahili* societies.

صِبْغَةَ اللّٰهِ ۚ وَمَنْ اَحْسَنُ مِنَ اللّٰهِ صِبْغَةً

***"The baptism of God — and who can baptize better than God?"*** *(2:138)*

# CHAPTER 8

## THE ISLAMIC CONCEPT AND CULTURE

In the sixth chapter we have shown that the first part of the first pillar of Islam is the dedication of one's life to God alone; this is the meaning of **"La ilaha illa Allah"**. The second part means that the way of this dedication comes from the Prophet Muhammad: **"Muhammadar Rasul Allah"** points to this fact. Complete submission to God comes by submitting to Him through belief, practice and in law. No Muslim can believe that another being can be a 'deity', nor can he believe that one can 'worship' a creature of God or that he can be given a position of 'sovereignty'. We explained in that chapter the meaning of worship, belief and sovereignty. In what follows we will show the true meaning of sovereignty and its relationship to culture.

In the Islamic concept, the sovereignty of God means not merely that one should derive all legal injunctions from God and judge according to these injunctions; in Islam the meaning of the '**Shari'ah**' is not limited to mere legal injunctions, but includes the principles of administration, its system and its modes. This narrow meaning (i.e., that the **Shari'ah** is limited to legal injunctions) does not apply to the **Shari'ah** nor does it correspond to the Islamic concept. By 'the **Shari'ah of God is meant everything legislated by God for ordering man's life; it includes the principles of belief, principles of administration and justice, principles of morality and human relationships, and principles of knowledge.**

The **Shari'ah** includes the Islamic beliefs and concepts and their implications concerning the attributes of God, the nature of life, what is apparent and what is hidden in it, the nature of man, and the interrelationships among these. Similarly, it includes political, social and economic affairs and their principles, with the intent that they reflect complete submission to God alone. It also includes legal matters (this is what today is referred to as the '**Shari'ah**', while the true meaning of the '**Shari'ah** in

Islam is entirely different). It deals with the morals, manners, values and standards of the society, according to which persons, actions and events are measured. It also deals with all aspects of knowledge and principles of art and science. In all these guidante from God is needed, just as it is needed in legal matters.

We have discussed the sovereignty of God in relation to government and the legal system, and also in relation to matters of morals, human relationships, and values and standards which prevail in a society. The point to note was that the values and standards, morals and manners, are all based on the beliefs and concepts prevalent in the society and are derived from the same Divine source from which beliefs are derived.

The thing which will appear strange, not only to the common man but also to writers about Islam, is our turning to Islam and to the Divine source for guidance in spheres of science and art.

A book has already been published on the subject of art in which it has been pointed out that all artistic efforts are but a reflection of a man's concepts, beliefs and intuitions; they reflect whatever pictures of life and the world are found in a man's intuition. All these affairs are not only governed by the Islamic concepts, but, in fact, this concept is a motivating power for a Muslim's creativity. The Islamic concept of the universe defines man's relationship to the rest of the universe and to his Creator. Its basic subject is the nature of man and his position in the universe, the purpose of his life, his function, and the true value of his life. These are all included in the Islamic concept, which is not merely an abstract idea but is a living, active motivating force which influences man's emotions and actions.[18]

In short, the question of art and literary thought and its relationship to Divine guidance requires a detailed discussion, and, as we have stated before, this discussion will appear strange not only to educated people but even to those Muslims who believe in the sovereignty of God in matters of law.

* * *

A Muslim cannot go to any source other than God for guidance in matters of faith, in the concept of life, acts of worship, morals and human affairs, values and standards, principles of economics and — political affairs and interpretation of historical processes. It is, therefore, his duty that he should learn all these from a Muslim whose piety and character, belief and action, are beyond reproach.

---

18. The book, **The Principles of Islamic Art**, by Muhammad Qutb.

However, a Muslim can go to a Muslim or to a non — Muslim to learn abstract sciences such as chemistry, physics, biology, astronomy, medicine, industry, agriculture, administration (limited to its technical aspects), technology, military arts and similar sciences and arts; although the fundamental principle is that when the Muslim community comes into existence it should provide experts in all these fields in abundance, as all these sciences and arts are a sufficient obligation (Fard al-Kifayah) on Muslims (that is to say, there ought to be a sufficient number of people who specialize in these various sciences and arts to satisfy the needs of the community). If a proper atmosphere is not provided under which these sciences and arts develop in a Muslim society, the whole society will be considered sinful; but as long as these conditions are not attained, it is permitted for a Muslim to learn them from a Muslim or a non — Muslim and to gain experience under his direction, without any distinction of religion. These are those affairs which are included in the Hadith, "You know best the affairs of your business". These sciences are not related to the basic concepts of a Muslim about life, the universe, man, the purpose of his creation, his responsibilities, his relationship with the physical world and with the Creator; these are also not related to the principles of law, the rules and regulations which order the lives of individuals and groups, nor are they related to morals, manners, traditions, habits, values and standards which prevail in the society and which give the society its shape and form. Thus there is no danger that a Muslim, by learning these sciences from a non — Muslim, will distort his belief or will return to ***Jahiliyyah***.

But as far as the interpretation of human endeavour is concerned, whether this endeavour be individual or collective, this relates to theories of the nature of man and of the historical processes. Similarly, the explanation of the origin of the universe, the origin of the life of man, are part of metaphysics (not related to the abstract sciences such as chemistry, physics, astronomy or medicine, etc.); and thus their position is similar to legal matters, rules and regulations which order human life. These indirectly affect man's beliefs; it is therefore not permissible for a Muslim to learn them from anyone other than a God — fearing and pious Muslim, who knows that guidance in these matters comes from God. The main purpose is, a Muslim should realize, that all these affairs are related to his faith, and that to seek guidance from God in these matters is a necessary consequence of the faith in the Oneness of God and the Messengership of Muhammad.

However, a Muslim can study all the opinions and thoughts of ***jahili*** writers, not from the point of view of constructing his own beliefs and concepts, but for the purpose of knowing the deviations adopted by

***Jahiliyyah***, so that he may know how to correct these man — made deviations in the light of the true Islamic belief and rebut them according to the sound principles of the Islamic teachings.

Philosophy, the interpretation of history, psychology (except for those observations and experimental results which are not part of anyone's opinion) ethics, theology and comparative religion, sociology (excluding statistics and observations) — all these sciences have a direction which in the past or the present has been influenced by ***jahili*** beliefs and traditions. That is why all these sciences come into conflict, explicitly or implicitly, with the fundamentals of any religion, and especially with Islam.

The situation concerning these areas of human thought and knowledge is not the same as with physics, chemistry, astronomy, biology, medicine, etc. — as long as these lastmentioned sciences limit themselves to practical experiments and their results, and do not go beyond their scope into speculative philosophy. For example, Darwinist biology goes beyond the scope of its observations, without any rhyme or reason and only for the sake of expressing an opinion, in making the assumption that to explain the beginning of life and its evolution there is no need to assume a power outside the physical world.

Concerning these matters, the true guidance from his Sustainer is sufficient for a Muslim. This guidance toward belief and complete submission to God alone is so superior to all man's speculative attempts in these affairs that they appear utterly ridiculous and absurd.

The statement that "Culture is/the human heritage" and that it has no country, nationality or religion is correct only in relation to science and technology — as long as we do not jump the boundary of these sciences and delve into metaphysical interpretations, and start explaining the purpose of man and his historical role in philosophical terms, even explaining away art and literature and human intuition philosophically. Beyond this limited meaning, this statement about culture is one of the tricks played by world Jewry, whose purpose is to eliminate all limitations, especially the limitations imposed by, faith and religion, so that the Jews may penetrate into body politic of the whole world and then may be free to perpetuate their evil designs. At the top of the list of these activities is usury, the aim of which is that all the wealth of mankind end up in the hands of Jewish financial institutions which run on interest.

However, Islam considers that — excepting the abstract sciences and their practical applications — there are two kinds of culture; the Islamic culture, which is based on the Islamic concept, and the ***jahili*** culture, which manifests itself in various modes of living which are nevertheless all based on one thing, and that is giving human thought the status of a god so that its truth or falsity is not to be judged according to God's guidance. The Islamic culture is concerned with all theoretical and practical affairs, and it contains principles, methods and characteristics which gurantee the development and perpetuation of all cultural activities.

One ought to remember the fact that the experimental method, which is the dynamic spirit of modern Europe's industrial culture, did not originate in Europe but originated in the Islamic universities of Andalusia and of the East. The principle of the experimental method was an offshoot of the Islamic concept and its explanations of the physical world, its phenomena, its forces and its secrets. Later, by adopting the experimental method, Europe entered into the period of scientific revival, which led it step by step to great scientific heights. Meanwhile, the Muslim world gradually drifted away from Islam, as a consequence of which the scientific movement first became inert and later ended completely. Some of the causes which led to this state of inertia were internal to the Muslim society and some were external, such as the invasions of the Muslim world by the Christians and Zionists. Europe removed the foundation of Islamic belief from the methodology of the empirical sciences, and finally, when Europe rebelled against the Church, which in the name of God oppressed the common people, it deprived the empirical sciences of their Islamic method of relating them to God's guidance.

Thus the entire basis of European thought became ***jahili*** and completely estranged from the Islamic concept, and even became contradictory and conflicting with it. It is necessary for a Muslim, therefore, to return to the guidance of God in order to learn the Islamic concept of life — on his own, if possible, or otherwise to seek knowledge from a God — fearing Muslim whose piety and faith are reliable.

* * *

In Islam the saying, "Seek knowledge from the one who knows", is not acceptable with respect to those sciences which relate to faith, religion, morals and values, customs and habits, and all those matters which concern human relationships.

No doubt Islam permits a Muslim to learn chemistry, physics, astronomy, medicine, technology and agriculture, administration and similar technical sciences from a non — Muslim or from a Muslim who is not pious — and this under the condition that no God — fearing Muslim scientists are available to teach these sciences. This is the situation which exists now, because

Muslims have drifted away from their religion and their way of life, and have forgotten that Islam appointed them as representatives of God and made them responsible for learning all the sciences and developing various capabilities to fulfill this high position which God has granted them. But Islam does not permit Muslims to learn the principles of their faith, the implications of their concept, the interpretation of the Qur'an, Hadith, the Prophet — peace be on him — the philosophy of history, the traditions of their society, the constitution of their government, the form of their politics, and similar branches of knowledge, from non — Islamic sources or from anyone other than a pious Muslim whose faith and religious knowledge is known to be reliable.

The person who is writing these lines has spent forty years of his life in reading books and in research in almost all aspects of human knowledge. He specialized in some branches of knowledge and he studied others due to personal interest. Then he turned to the fountainhead of his faith. He came to feel that whatever he had read so far was as nothing in comparison to what he found here. He does not regret spending forty years of his life in the pursuit of these sciences, because he came to know the nature of ***Jahiliyyah***, its deviations, its errors and its ignorance, as well as its pomp and noise, its arrogant and boastful claims. Finally, he was convinced that a Muslim cannot combine these two sources — the source of Divine guidance and the source of **Jahiliyyah** — for his education.

Even then, this is not my personal opinion; this is a grave matter to be decided merely by some person's opinion, and the question of depending on a Muslim's opinion does not arise when the Divine standard provides us a way to judge the matter. This is the decision of God and His Messenger — peace be on him — and we refer it to them. We refer it to them in the same manner as is befitting for a Believer, as all controversial decisions ought to be referred to the judgement of God and His Prophet — peace be on him.

God Most High says in general terms concerning the ultimate aims of the Jews and Christians against Muslims:

وَدَّ كَثِيرٌ مِّنْ أَهْلِ الْكِتَٰبِ لَوْ يَرُدُّونَكُم مِّنۢ بَعْدِ إِيمَٰنِكُمْ كُفَّارًا حَسَدًا
مِّنْ عِندِ أَنفُسِهِم مِّنۢ بَعْدِ مَا تَبَيَّنَ لَهُمُ الْحَقُّ ۖ فَاعْفُوا وَاصْفَحُوا حَتَّىٰ
يَأْتِيَ اللَّهُ بِأَمْرِهِ ۗ إِنَّ اللَّهَ عَلَىٰ كُلِّ شَيْءٍ قَدِيرٌ ﴿١٠٩﴾

***"Many among the People of the Book wish to turn you back from your faith toward unbelief,***

*due to their envy, even after the truth has been known to them; but forgive and excuse them until God brings about His decision. Indeed, God has power over everything."* *(2:109)*

وَلَنْ تَرْضٰى عَنْكَ الْيَهُوْدُ وَلَا النَّصٰرٰى حَتّٰى تَتَّبِعَ مِلَّتَهُمْ ؕ قُلْ اِنَّ هُدَى
اللّٰهِ هُوَ الْهُدٰى ؕ وَلَئِنِ اتَّبَعْتَ اَهْوَآءَهُمْ بَعْدَ الَّذِىْ جَآءَكَ مِنَ الْعِلْمِ ۙ مَا
لَكَ مِنَ اللّٰهِ مِنْ وَّلِىٍّ وَّلَا نَصِيْرٍ ﴿١٢٠﴾

*'The Jews and Christians will not be pleased with you unless you follow their way. Say: "Indeed, God's guidance is the true guidance'. And if, after this knowledge has come to you, you follow their desires, then you will find no helper or friend against God."* *(2:120)*

يٰۤاَيُّهَا الَّذِيْنَ اٰمَنُوْۤا اِنْ تُطِيْعُوْا فَرِيْقًا مِّنَ الَّذِيْنَ
اُوْتُوا الْكِتٰبَ يَرُدُّوْكُمْ بَعْدَ اِيْمَانِكُمْ كٰفِرِيْنَ ﴿١٠٠﴾

*"O you who believe! If you follow a party of the People of the Book, they will return you to the state of unbelief after you have believed."*

*(3:100)*

As reported by Hafiz Abu Y'ala, the Messenger of God peace be on him — said: "Do not ask the People of the Book about anything. They will not guide you, In fact, they are themselves misguided. If you listen to them, you might end up accepting some falsehood or denying some truth. By God, If Moses had been alive among you, he would not be permitted (by God) anything except to follow me."

After this warning to the Muslims from God concerning the ultimate designs of the Jews and Christians, it would be extremely short — sighted of us to fall into the illusion that when the Jews and Christians discuss Islamic beliefs or Islamic history, or when they make proposals concerning Muslim society or Muslim politics or economics, they will be 'doing it with good intentions, or with the welfare of the Muslims at heart, or in order to seek guidance and light. People who, after this clear statement from God, still think this way are indeed deluded.

Similarly, the saying of God Most High: "Say: 'Indeed, God's guidance is the true guidance", determines the unique source to which every Muslim should turn for guidance in all these affairs, as whatever is beyond God's guidance, is error and none other than He can guide, as is clear from the emphasis in the verse, "Say: 'Indeed, God's guidance is the true guidance". There is no ambiguity in the meaning of this verse and no other interpretation is possible.

There is also a decisive injunction to avoid a person who turns away from the remembrance of God and whose only object is this world. It is explained that such a person follows mere speculation — and a Muslim is forbidden to follow speculation — and he knows only what is apparent in the life of this world and does not possess the true knowledge.

فَأَعْرِضْ عَنْ مَّنْ تَوَلّٰى ۙ عَنْ ذِكْرِنَا وَلَمْ يُرِدْ اِلَّا الْحَيٰوةَ الدُّنْيَا ﴿٢٩﴾ ذٰلِكَ مَبْلَغُهُمْ مِّنَ
الْعِلْمِ ۭ اِنَّ رَبَّكَ هُوَ اَعْلَمُ بِمَنْ ضَلَّ عَنْ سَبِيْلِهٖ ۙ وَهُوَ اَعْلَمُ بِمَنِ اهْتَدٰى ﴿٣٠﴾

***"Avoid a person who has turned away from Our remembrance and does not desire anything beyond the life of this world, and this is the extent of his knowledge. Your Sustainer knows best who has gone astray from His path, and He knows best who is guided."*** ***(53:29-30)***

يَعْلَمُوْنَ ظَاهِرًا مِّنَ الْحَيٰوةِ الدُّنْيَا ۚ وَهُمْ عَنِ الْاٰخِرَةِ هُمْ غٰفِلُوْنَ ﴿٧﴾

***"They only know what is apparent in the life of this world, and are negligent of the Hereafter."***

***(30:7)***

A person who is negligent in remembering God and is completely occupied with the affairs of this life — and that is the case with all the 'scientists' of today — knows only what is apparent, and this is not the type of knowledge, for which a Muslim can rely completely on its possessor, except for what is permitted to be learned from them to the extent of technical knowledge. He should ignore their interpretations concerning psychological and conceptual matters. This is not that knowledge which is praised repeatedly in the Qur'an for example in the verse, "Are they equal-those who know and those who do not know"? Those who take such verses out of context and argue are in error. The complete verse in which this rhetorical question is posed is as follows:

اَمَّنْ هُوَ قَانِتٌ اٰنَاۗءَ الَّيْلِ سَاجِدًا وَّقَاۗىِٕمًا يَّحْذَرُ الْاٰخِرَةَ وَيَرْجُوْا رَحْمَةَ رَبِّهٖ ۭ قُلْ هَلْ
يَسْتَوِي الَّذِيْنَ يَعْلَمُوْنَ وَالَّذِيْنَ لَا يَعْلَمُوْنَ ۭ اِنَّمَا يَتَذَكَّرُ اُولُوا الْاَلْبَابِ ﴿٩﴾

> ***"... Or is he who is worshipful in the watches of the night, prostrating and standing, he being afraid of the Hereafter and hoping for the mercy of His Sustainer? Say: Are they equal-those who know and those who do not know? Indeed, the thinking persons take heed." (39:9)***

Only such a person who, in the darkness of the night, remaint worshipping, standing or prostrating, who fears the Hereafter, and hopes for the mercy of his Sustainer, is truly knowing, and it is his knowledge to which the above verse refers; that is to say, the knowledge which guides toward God and the remembrance of Him,. and not that knowledge which distorts human nature toward denial of God.

The sphere of knowledge is not limited to articles of faith, religious obligations, or laws about what is permissible and what is forbidden; its sphere is very wide. It includes all these and also the knowledge of natural laws and all matters concerning man's delegated role before God. However, any knowledge, the foundation of which is not based on faith, is outside the definition of that knowledge which is referred to in the Qur'an and the possessors of which are considered praiseworthy. There is a strong relationship between faith and all those sciences which deal with the universe and natural laws, such as astronomy, biology, physics, chemistry and geology. Alt these sciences lead man toward God, unless they are perverted by personal opinions and speculations, and presented devoid of the concept of God. Such a regrettable situation actually occurred in Europe. In fact, there came a time in European history when very painful and hateful differences arose between scientists and the oppressive Church; consequently the entire scientific movement in Europe started with Godlessness. This movement affected all aspects of life very deeply; in fact, it changed the entire character of European thought. The effect of this hostility of the scientific community toward the Church did not remain limited to the Church or to its beliefs, but was directed against all religion, so much so that all sciences turned against religion, whether they were speculative philosophy or technical or abstract sciences having nothing to do with religion.[19]

The Western ways of thought and all the sciences started on the foundation of these poisonous influences with an enmity toward all religion, and in particular with greater hostility toward Islam. This enmity toward Islam is

---

19. Refer to the chapter, "Al-Fisam al-Nakad", in the book **The Future Belongs to This Religion**.

especially pronounced and many times is the result of a well — thought — out scheme, the object of which is first to shake the foundations of Islamic beliefs and then gradually to demolish the structure of Muslim society.

If, in spite of knowing this, we rely on Western ways of thought, even in teaching the Islamic sciences, it will be an unforgiveable blindness on our part. Indeed, it becomes incumbent on us, while learning purely scientific or technological subjects for which we have no other sources except Western sources, to remain on guard and keep these sciences away from philosophical speculations, as these philosophical speculations are generally against religion and in particular against Islam. A slight influence from them can pollute the clear spring of Islam.

## CHAPTER 9

# A MUSLIM'S NATIONALITY AND HIS BELIEF

The day Islam gave a new concept of values and standards to mankind and showed the way to learn these values and standards, it also provided it with a new concept of human relationships. Islam came to return man to his Sustainer and to make His guidance the only source from which values and standards are to be obtained, as He is the Provider and Originator. All relationships ought to be based through Him, as we came into being through His will and shall return to Him.

Islam came to establish only one relationship which binds men together in the sight of God, and if this relationship is firmly established, then all other relationships based on blood or other considerations become eliminated.

لَا تَجِدُ قَوْمًا يُؤْمِنُونَ بِاللَّهِ وَالْيَوْمِ الْآخِرِ يُوَادُّونَ مَنْ حَادَّ اللَّهَ وَرَسُولَهُ
وَلَوْ كَانُوا آبَاءَهُمْ أَوْ أَبْنَاءَهُمْ أَوْ إِخْوَانَهُمْ أَوْ عَشِيرَتَهُمْ

***"You will not find the people who believe in God and the Hereafter taking as allies the enemies of God and His Prophet, whether they be their fathers or sons or brothers or fellow tribesmen."***

***(58:22)***

In the world there is only one party of God; all others are parties of Satan and rebellion.

الَّذِينَ آمَنُوا يُقَاتِلُونَ فِي سَبِيلِ اللَّهِ ۖ وَالَّذِينَ كَفَرُوا يُقَاتِلُونَ فِي سَبِيلِ
الطَّاغُوتِ فَقَاتِلُوا أَوْلِيَاءَ الشَّيْطَانِ ۖ إِنَّ كَيْدَ الشَّيْطَانِ كَانَ ضَعِيفًا ﴿٧٦﴾

***"Those who believe fight in the cause of God, and those who disbelieve fight in the cause of***

***rebellion. Then fight the allies of Satan; indeed, Satan's strategy is weak."*** ***(4:76)***

There is only one way to reach God; all other ways do not lead to Him.

وَأَنَّ هَٰذَا صِرَاطِي مُسْتَقِيمًا فَاتَّبِعُوهُ ۖ وَلَا تَتَّبِعُوا السُّبُلَ فَتَفَرَّقَ بِكُمْ
عَن سَبِيلِهِ

***"This is My straight path. Then follow it, and do not follow other ways which will scatter you from His path."*** ***(6:153)***

For human life, there is only one true system, and that is Islam; all other systems are **Jahillyyah**.

أَفَحُكْمَ الْجَاهِلِيَّةِ يَبْغُونَ ۚ وَمَنْ أَحْسَنُ مِنَ اللَّهِ حُكْمًا لِّقَوْمٍ يُوقِنُونَ ﴿٥٠﴾

***"Do they want a judgement of the Days of Ignorance? Yet who is better in judgement than God, for a people having sure faith?*** ***(5:50)***

There is only one law which ought to be followed, and that is the **Shari'ah** from God; anything elsë is mere emotionalism and impulsiyeness.

ثُمَّ جَعَلْنَاكَ عَلَىٰ شَرِيعَةٍ مِّنَ الْأَمْرِ فَاتَّبِعْهَا وَلَا تَتَّبِعْ أَهْوَاءَ الَّذِينَ لَا يَعْلَمُونَ ﴿١٨﴾

***"We have set you on a way ordained (by God); then follow it, and do not follow the desires of those who have no knowledge."*** ***(45:18)***

The truth is one and indivisible; anything different from it is error.

فَذَٰلِكُمُ اللَّهُ رَبُّكُمُ الْحَقُّ ۖ فَمَاذَا بَعْدَ الْحَقِّ إِلَّا الضَّلَالُ ۖ فَأَنَّىٰ تُصْرَفُونَ ﴿٣٢﴾

***"Is anything left besides error, beyond the truth? Then to which do you go?"*** ***(10:32)***

There is only one place on earth which can be called the home of Islam (**Dar-ul-Islam**), and it is that place where the Islamic state is established and the **Shari'ah** is the authority and God's limits are observed, and where all the Muslims administer the affairs of the state with mutual consulation. The rest of the world is the home of hostility (**Dar-ul-Harb**). A Muslim can have only two possible relations with Dar-ul-Harb: peace with a contractual agreement, or war. A country with which there is a treaty will not be considered the home of Islam.

إِنَّ الَّذِينَ آمَنُوا وَهَاجَرُوا وَجَاهَدُوا بِأَمْوَالِهِمْ وَأَنفُسِهِمْ فِي سَبِيلِ اللَّهِ وَالَّذِينَ
آوَوا وَّنَصَرُوا أُولَٰئِكَ بَعْضُهُمْ أَوْلِيَاءُ بَعْضٍ ۚ وَالَّذِينَ آمَنُوا وَلَمْ يُهَاجِرُوا مَا لَكُم
مِّن وَلَايَتِهِم مِّن شَيْءٍ حَتَّىٰ يُهَاجِرُوا ۚ وَإِنِ اسْتَنصَرُوكُمْ فِي الدِّينِ
فَعَلَيْكُمُ النَّصْرُ إِلَّا عَلَىٰ قَوْمٍ بَيْنَكُمْ وَبَيْنَهُم مِّيثَاقٌ ۗ وَاللَّهُ بِمَا تَعْمَلُونَ
بَصِيرٌ ﴿٧٢﴾ وَالَّذِينَ كَفَرُوا بَعْضُهُمْ أَوْلِيَاءُ بَعْضٍ ۚ إِلَّا تَفْعَلُوهُ تَكُن فِتْنَةٌ فِي
الْأَرْضِ وَفَسَادٌ كَبِيرٌ ﴿٧٣﴾ وَالَّذِينَ آمَنُوا وَهَاجَرُوا وَجَاهَدُوا فِي سَبِيلِ اللَّهِ وَالَّذِينَ
آوَوا وَّنَصَرُوا أُولَٰئِكَ هُمُ الْمُؤْمِنُونَ حَقًّا ۚ لَّهُم مَّغْفِرَةٌ وَرِزْقٌ كَرِيمٌ ﴿٧٤﴾
وَالَّذِينَ آمَنُوا مِن بَعْدُ وَهَاجَرُوا وَجَاهَدُوا مَعَكُمْ فَأُولَٰئِكَ مِنكُمْ ۚ

> ***"Those who believed, and migrated, and strove with their wealth and their persons in the cause of God, and those who gave them refuge and helped them, are the protectors of each other. As to those who believed but did not emigrate, you have no responsibility for their protection until they emigrate; but if they ask your help in religion, it is your duty to help them, except against a people between whom and you there is a treaty; and God sees whatever you do. Those who disbelieve are the allies of each other. If you do not do this, there will be oppression in the earth and a great disturbance. Those who believe, and migrate, and fight in the cause of God, and those who give them refuge and help them, are in truth Believers. For them is forgiveness and generous provision. And those who accept Faith afterwards and migrate and strive along with you, they are of you."*** (8:72-75)

Islam came with this total guidance and decisive teaching. It came to elevate man above, and release him from, the bonds of the earth and soil, the bonds of flesh and blood — which are also the bonds of the earth and soil. A Muslim has no country except that part of the earth where the **Shari'ah** of God is established and human relationships are based on the foundation of relationship with God; a Muslim has no nationality except his belief, which makes him a member of the Muslim community in **Dar-ul-Islam**; a Muslim has no relatives except those who share the belief in

God, and thus a bond is established between him and other Believers through their relationship with God.

A Muslim has no relationship with his mother, father, brother, wife and other family members except through their relationship with the Creator, and then they are also joined through blood.

يَٰٓأَيُّهَا النَّاسُ اتَّقُوا رَبَّكُمُ الَّذِى خَلَقَكُم مِّن نَّفْسٍ وَّاحِدَةٍ وَّخَلَقَ
مِنْهَا زَوْجَهَا وَبَثَّ مِنْهُمَا رِجَالًا كَثِيرًا وَّنِسَآءً ۚ وَاتَّقُوا اللَّهَ الَّذِى
تَسَآءَلُونَ بِهِۦ وَالْأَرْحَامَ

> ***"O mankind, remain conscious of your Sustainer, Who created you from one soul and created from its mate, and from the two of them scattered a great many men and women. Remain conscious of God, from Whose authority you make demands, and reverence the wombs (from which you were born).*** *(4:1)*

However, Divine relationship does not prohibit a Muslim from treating his parents with kindness and consideration, in spite of differences of belief, as long as they do not join the front lines of the enemies of Islam. However, if they openly declare their alliance with the enemies of Islam, then all the filial relationships of a Muslim are cut off and he is not bound to be kind and considerate to them. Abdullah, son of Abdullah bin Ubayy, has presented us with a bright example in this respect.

Ibn Jarir, on the authority of IbnZiad, has reported that the Prophet called Abdullah, son of Abdullah bin Ubayy, and said, "Do you know what your father said?" Abdullah asked. "May my, parents be a ransom for you; what did my father say?" The prophet replied, "He said, 'If we return to Medina (from the battle), the one with honour will throw out the one who is despised." Abdullah then said, "O Messenger of God, by God, he told the truth. You are the one with honour and he is the one who is despised. 0 Messenger of God, the people of Medina know that before you came to Medina, no one was more obedient to his father than I was. But now, if it is the pleasure of God and His Prophet that I cut off his head, then I shall do so." The Prophet replied, "No". When the Muslims returned to Medina, Abdullah stood, in front of the gate with his sword drawn over his father's head, telling him, "Did you say that if we return to Medina then the one with honor will throw out the one who is despised?

By God, now you will know whether you have honor, or God's Messenger! By God, until God and His Messenger give permission, you cannot enter Medina, nor will you have refuge from me!" IbnUbayy cried aloud and said twice, "People of Khazraj — , see how my son is preventing me from entering my home!" But his son Abdullah kept repeating that unless the Prophet gave permission he would not let him enter Medina. Hearing this noise, some people gathered around and started pleading with Abdullah, but he stood his ground. Some people went to the Prophet and reported this incident. He told them, "Tell Abdullah to let his father enter". When Abdullah got this message, he then told his father, "Since the Prophet had given permission, you can enter now."

When the relationship of the belief is established, whether there by any relationship of blood or not, the Believers become like brothers. God Most High says, "Indeed, the Believers are brothers," which is a limitation as well as a pres cription. He also says:

إِنَّ الَّذِينَ آمَنُوا وَهَاجَرُوا وَجَاهَدُوا بِأَمْوَالِهِمْ وَأَنفُسِهِمْ فِي سَبِيلِ اللَّهِ
وَالَّذِينَ آوَوا وَّنَصَرُوا أُولَٰئِكَ بَعْضُهُمْ أَوْلِيَاءُ بَعْضٍ

***"Those who believed, and migrated, and strove with their wealth and their persons in the cause of God, and those who gave them refuge and helped them, are the protectors of each other."***
*(8:72)*

The protection which is referred to in this verse is not limited to a single generation but encompasses future generations as well, thus linking the future generations with the past generation in a sacred and eternal bond of love, loyalty and kindness.

وَالَّذِينَ تَبَوَّءُوا الدَّارَ وَالْإِيمَانَ مِن قَبْلِهِمْ يُحِبُّونَ مَنْ هَاجَرَ إِلَيْهِمْ وَلَا
يَجِدُونَ فِي صُدُورِهِمْ حَاجَةً مِّمَّا أُوتُوا وَيُؤْثِرُونَ عَلَىٰ أَنفُسِهِمْ وَلَوْ كَانَ
بِهِمْ خَصَاصَةٌ ۚ وَمَن يُوقَ شُحَّ نَفْسِهِ فَأُولَٰئِكَ هُمُ الْمُفْلِحُونَ ﴿٩﴾ وَالَّذِينَ جَاءُوا
مِن بَعْدِهِمْ يَقُولُونَ رَبَّنَا اغْفِرْ لَنَا وَلِإِخْوَانِنَا الَّذِينَ سَبَقُونَا بِالْإِيمَانِ وَلَا تَجْعَلْ
فِي قُلُوبِنَا غِلًّا لِّلَّذِينَ آمَنُوا رَبَّنَا إِنَّكَ رَءُوفٌ رَّحِيمٌ ﴿١٠﴾

***"Those who lived (in Medina) before the Emigrants and believed, love the Emigrants and do not find in their hearts any grudge when thou givest***

> *them something, but give them preference over themselves, even though they may be poor. Indeed, the ones who restrain themselves from greed , achieve prosperity. Those who came after them (the Emigrants) say; 'Our Lord! Forgive us and our brothers who entered the Faith before us, and leave not in our hearts any grievance against those who believe. Our Lord! You are indeed Most Kind, Most Merciful."* *(59:9-10)*

God Most High has related the stories of earlier Prophets in the Qur'an as an example for the Believers. In various periods the Prophets of God lighted the flame of faith and guided the Believers.

وَنَادٰى نُوْحٌ رَّبَّهٗ فَقَالَ رَبِّ اِنَّ ابْنِيْ مِنْ اَهْلِيْ وَاِنَّ وَعْدَكَ الْحَقُّ وَاَنْتَ اَحْكَمُ
الْحٰكِمِيْنَ ﴿۴۵﴾ قَالَ يٰنُوْحُ اِنَّهٗ لَيْسَ مِنْ اَهْلِكَ ۚ اِنَّهٗ عَمَلٌ غَيْرُ صَالِحٍ ۖ فَلَا تَسْـَٔلْنِ مَا
لَيْسَ لَكَ بِهٖ عِلْمٌ ۭ اِنِّيْٓ اَعِظُكَ اَنْ تَكُوْنَ مِنَ الْجٰهِلِيْنَ ﴿۴۶﴾ قَالَ رَبِّ اِنِّيْٓ اَعُوْذُ بِكَ
اَنْ اَسْـَٔلَكَ مَا لَيْسَ لِيْ بِهٖ عِلْمٌ ۭ وَاِلَّا تَغْفِرْ لِيْ وَتَرْحَمْنِيْٓ اَكُنْ مِّنَ الْخٰسِرِيْنَ ﴿۴۷﴾

> *"And Noah called upon his Lord and said, 'O my Lord, surely my son is of my family, and Your promise is true, and You are the Justest of Judges'. He said, 'O Noah, he is not of your family, as his conduct is unrighteous; so do not ask of me that of which you have no knowledge. I give you the counsel not to act like the ignorant.' Noah said, 'O my Lord, I seek refuge with You lest I ask You for that of which I have no knowledge, and unles You forgive me and have mercy on me, I shall be lost".* *(11:45-47)*

وَاِذِ ابْتَلٰٓى اِبْرٰهٖمَ رَبُّهٗ بِكَلِمٰتٍ فَاَتَمَّهُنَّ ۭ قَالَ اِنِّىْ جَاعِلُكَ لِلنَّاسِ اِمَامًا ۭ
قَالَ وَمِنْ ذُرِّيَّتِيْ ۭ قَالَ لَا يَنَالُ عَهْدِي الظّٰلِمِيْنَ ﴿۱۲۴﴾

> *"And when his Lord tried Abraham with certain commands which he fulfilled, he said, 'I will make you a leader of people'. He said, 'And also those from among my offspring'? He answered, 'My promise does not extend to the evildoers".*
>
> *(1:124)*

وَإِذْ قَالَ إِبْرٰهِيمُ رَبِّ اجْعَلْ هٰذَا بَلَدًا اٰمِنًا وَّارْزُقْ اَهْلَهٗ مِنَ الثَّمَرٰتِ مَنْ
اٰمَنَ مِنْهُمْ بِاللّٰهِ وَالْيَوْمِ الْاٰخِرِ ۗ قَالَ وَمَنْ كَفَرَ فَاُمَتِّعُهٗ قَلِيْلًا ثُمَّ اَضْطَرُّهٗۤ
اِلٰى عَذَابِ النَّارِ ۗ وَبِئْسَ الْمَصِيْرُ ﴿١٢٦﴾

***"And when Abraham said, 'My Lord! Make this a city of peace and feed its people with fruits, such of them as believe in God and the Last Day'. He said, 'And those who reject faith, I will grant them their pleasure for a while, but will eventually drive them to the chastisement of the Fire. What an evil destination!"*** *(2:126)*

When the Prophet Abraham saw his father and his people persistent in their error, he turned away from them and said,

وَاَعْتَزِلُكُمْ وَمَا تَدْعُوْنَ مِنْ دُوْنِ اللّٰهِ وَاَدْعُوْا رَبِّيْ ۖ
عَسٰۤى اَلَّاۤ اَكُوْنَ بِدُعَآءِ رَبِّيْ شَقِيًّا ﴿٤٨﴾

***"I leave you and those upon whom you call besides God. I will only call upon my Sustainer, and hope that my Lord will not disappoint me."*** *(19:48)*

In relating the story of Abraham and his people, God has highlighted those aspects which are to be an exampie for the Believers.

قَدْ كَانَتْ لَكُمْ اُسْوَةٌ حَسَنَةٌ فِيْۤ اِبْرٰهِيْمَ وَالَّذِيْنَ مَعَهٗ ۚ اِذْ قَالُوْا لِقَوْمِهِمْ اِنَّا بُرَءٰٓؤُا
مِنْكُمْ وَمِمَّا تَعْبُدُوْنَ مِنْ دُوْنِ اللّٰهِ كَفَرْنَا بِكُمْ وَبَدَا بَيْنَنَا وَبَيْنَكُمُ الْعَدَاوَةُ
وَالْبَغْضَآءُ اَبَدًا حَتّٰى تُؤْمِنُوْا بِاللّٰهِ وَحْدَهٗۤ

***"Indeed, Abraham and his companions are an example for you, when they told their people, 'We have nothing to do wi th you and with whatever you worship besides God. We reject them; and now there is perpetual enmity and anger between you and us unless you believe in One God."*** *(60:4)*

When those young and courageous friends who are known as the Companions of the Cave saw this same rejection among their family and tribe, they left them all, migrated from their country, and ran toward their Sustainer so that they could live as His servants.

نَحْنُ نَقُصُّ عَلَيْكَ نَبَأَهُمْ بِالْحَقِّ ۚ إِنَّهُمْ فِتْيَةٌ آمَنُوا بِرَبِّهِمْ وَزِدْنَاهُمْ هُدًى ﴿١٣﴾
وَرَبَطْنَا عَلَىٰ قُلُوبِهِمْ إِذْ قَامُوا فَقَالُوا رَبُّنَا رَبُّ السَّمَاوَاتِ وَالْأَرْضِ لَنْ نَدْعُوَ مِنْ
دُونِهِ إِلَٰهًا ۖ لَقَدْ قُلْنَا إِذًا شَطَطًا ﴿١٤﴾ هَٰؤُلَاءِ قَوْمُنَا اتَّخَذُوا مِنْ دُونِهِ آلِهَةً ۖ لَوْلَا
يَأْتُونَ عَلَيْهِمْ بِسُلْطَانٍ بَيِّنٍ ۖ فَمَنْ أَظْلَمُ مِمَّنِ افْتَرَىٰ عَلَى اللَّهِ كَذِبًا ﴿١٥﴾ وَإِذِ
اعْتَزَلْتُمُوهُمْ وَمَا يَعْبُدُونَ إِلَّا اللَّهَ فَأْوُوا إِلَى الْكَهْفِ يَنْشُرْ لَكُمْ رَبُّكُمْ مِنْ
رَحْمَتِهِ وَيُهَيِّئْ لَكُمْ مِنْ أَمْرِكُمْ مِرْفَقًا ﴿١٦﴾

*"They were youths who believed in their Lord, and We advanced them in guidance. We gave strength to hearts, so that they stood up and said, 'Our Lord is the Lord of the heavens and the earth. We shall not call upon any god apart from Him. If we did, we should indeed have said an awful thing. These our people have taken for worship gods other than Him. Why do they not bring a clear proof for what they do? Who can be more wrong than such as invert a falsehood against God? So, when you turn away from them and the things they worship other than God, take refuge in the cave. Your Lord will shower mercies on you and will provide ease and comfort for, your affairs"! (18:13-16)*

The wife of Noah and the wife of Lot were separated from their husbands only because their beliefs were different.

ضَرَبَ اللَّهُ مَثَلًا لِلَّذِينَ كَفَرُوا امْرَأَتَ نُوحٍ وَامْرَأَتَ لُوطٍ ۖ كَانَتَا تَحْتَ
عَبْدَيْنِ مِنْ عِبَادِنَا صَالِحَيْنِ فَخَانَتَاهُمَا فَلَمْ يُغْنِيَا عَنْهُمَا مِنَ اللَّهِ شَيْئًا
وَقِيلَ ادْخُلَا النَّارَ مَعَ الدَّاخِلِينَ ﴿١٠﴾

*"God gives as an example for the unbelievers the wife of Noah and the wife of Lot. They were married to two of Our righteous servants; but they were false to their husbands, and they profited nothing before God on their account, but were told, 'Enter you both into the fire along with those who enter it." (66:10)*

Then there is another kind of example in the wife of Pharoah.

وَضَرَبَ اللّٰهُ مَثَلًا لِّلَّذِيْنَ اٰمَنُوا امْرَاَتَ فِرْعَوْنَ ۘ اِذْ قَالَتْ رَبِّ ابْنِ لِيْ عِنْدَكَ
بَيْتًا فِي الْجَنَّةِ وَنَجِّنِيْ مِنْ فِرْعَوْنَ وَعَمَلِهٖ وَنَجِّنِيْ مِنَ الْقَوْمِ الظّٰلِمِيْنَ ﴿١١﴾

***"And God gives as an example to those who believe the wife of Pharoah. Behold, she said, 'My Lord, build for me in nearness to You a mansion in heaven, and save me from Pharoah and his doings, and save me from those who do wrong." (66:11)***

The Qur'an also describes examples of different kinds of relationships. In the story of Noah we have an example of the paternal relationship; in the story of Abraham, an example of the son and of the country; in the story of the Companions of the Cave a comprehensive example of relatives, tribe and home country. In the 'stories of Noah, Lot and Pharoah there is an example of marital relationships.

After a description of the lives of the great Prophets and their relationships, we now turn" to the Middle Community, that is, that of the early Muslims. We find similar examples and experiences in this community in great numbers. This community followed the Divine path which God has chosen for the Believers. When the relationship of common belief was broken — in other words, when the very first relationship joining one man with another was broken, — then persons of the same family or tribe were divided into different groups. God Most High says in praise of the Believers:

لَا تَجِدُ قَوْمًا يُّؤْمِنُوْنَ بِاللّٰهِ وَالْيَوْمِ الْاٰخِرِ يُوَآدُّوْنَ مَنْ حَآدَّ اللّٰهَ وَرَسُوْلَهٗ وَلَوْ كَانُوْٓا
اٰبَآءَهُمْ اَوْ اَبْنَآءَهُمْ اَوْ اِخْوَانَهُمْ اَوْ عَشِيْرَتَهُمْ ؕ اُولٰٓئِكَ كَتَبَ فِيْ قُلُوْبِهِمُ الْاِيْمَانَ
وَاَيَّدَهُمْ بِرُوْحٍ مِّنْهُ ؕ وَيُدْخِلُهُمْ جَنّٰتٍ تَجْرِيْ مِنْ تَحْتِهَا الْاَنْهٰرُ خٰلِدِيْنَ فِيْهَا ؕ رَضِيَ
اللّٰهُ عَنْهُمْ وَرَضُوْا عَنْهُ ؕ اُولٰٓئِكَ حِزْبُ اللّٰهِ ؕ اَلَآ اِنَّ حِزْبَ اللّٰهِ هُمُ الْمُفْلِحُوْنَ ﴿٢٢﴾

***"You will not find any people who believe in God and the Last Day loving those who fight God and His Messenger, even though they be their fathers, or their sons, or their brothers, or their kindred. These are the people on whose hearts God has imprinted faith and strengthened them with a spirit from Himself. And He will admit***

> ***them to Gardens beneath which rivers flow, to dwell therein. God will be well — pleased with them and they with Him. They are the party of God; truly the party of God will prosper.'***
>
> *(58:22)*

We see that the blood relationships between Muhammad — peace be on him — and his uncle Abu Lahab and his cousin Abu jahl were broken, and that the Emigrants from Mecca were fighting against their families and relatives and were in the front lines of Badr, while on the other hand their relations with the Helpers of Medina became strengthened on the basis of a common faith. They became like brother's, even more than blood relatives. This relationship established a new brotherhood of Muslims in which — were included Arabs and non — Arabs. Suhaib from Rome and Bilal from Abyssinia and Selman from Persia were all brothers. There was no tribal partisanship among them. The pride of lineage was ended, the voice of nationalism was silenced, and the Messenger of God addressed then "Get rid of these partisanships; these are foul things", and "He is not one of us who calls toward partisanship, who fights for partisanship, and who dies for partisanship."

Thus this partisanship — the partisanship of lineage — ended; and this slogan — the slogan of race — died; and this pride — the pride of nationality — vanished; and man's spirit. soared to higher horizons, freed from the bondage of flesh and blood and the pride of soil and country. From that day, the Muslim's country has not been a piece of land, but the homeland of Islam (**Dar-ul-Islam**) — the homeland where faith rules and the **Shari'ah** of God holds sway, the homeland in which he took refuge and which he defended, and in trying to extend it, he become martyred. This Islamic homeland is a refuge for any who accepts the Islamic **Shari'ah** to be the law of the state, as is the case with the **Dhimmies**. But any place where the Islamic **Shari'ah** is not enforced and where Islam is not dominant becomes the home of Hostility (**Dar-ul-Harb**) for both the Muslim and the **Dhimmi**. A Muslim will remain prepared to fight against it, whether it be his birthplace or a place where his relatives reside or where his property or any other material interests are located.

And thus Muhammad — peace be on him — fought against the city of Mecca, although it was his birthplace, and his relatives lived there, and he and his Companions had houses and property there which they had left when they migrated; yet the soil of Mecca did not become **Dar-ul-Islam** for him and his followers until it surrendered to Islam and the **Shari'ah** became operative in it.

* * *

This, and only this, is Islam. Islam is not a few words pronounced by the tongue, or birth in a country called Islamic, or an inheritance from a Muslim father.

فَلَا وَرَبِّكَ لَا يُؤْمِنُونَ حَتَّىٰ يُحَكِّمُوكَ فِيمَا شَجَرَ بَيْنَهُمْ ثُمَّ لَا يَجِدُوا فِي
أَنفُسِهِمْ حَرَجًا مِّمَّا قَضَيْتَ وَيُسَلِّمُوا تَسْلِيمًا ٦٥

***"No, by your Sustainer, they have not believed until they make you the arbiter of their disputes, and then do not find any grievance against your decision but submit with full submission."*** *(4:65)*

Only this is Islam, and only this is **Dar-ul-Islam** — not the soil, not the race, not the lineage, not the tribe, and not the family.

Islam freed all humanity from the ties of the earth so that they might soar toward the skies, and freed them from the chains of blood relationships — the biological chains — so that they might rise above the angels.

The homeland of the Muslim, in which he lives and which he defends, is not a piece of land; the nationality of the Muslim, by which he is identified, is not the nationality determined by a government; the family of the Muslim, in which he finds solace and which he defends, is not blood relationships; the flag of the Muslim, which he honors and under which he is martyred, is not the flag of a country; and the victory of the Muslim, which he celebrates and for which he is thankful to God, is not a military victory. It is what God has described:

إِذَا جَاءَ نَصْرُ اللَّهِ وَالْفَتْحُ ١ وَرَأَيْتَ النَّاسَ يَدْخُلُونَ فِي دِينِ اللَّهِ أَفْوَاجًا ٢
فَسَبِّحْ بِحَمْدِ رَبِّكَ وَاسْتَغْفِرْهُ ۚ إِنَّهُ كَانَ تَوَّابًا ٣

***"When God's help and victory comes, and thou seest people entering into God's religion in multitudes, then celebrate the praises of thy Lord and ask His forgiveness. Indeed, He is the Acceptor of Repentance."*** *(110:1-3)*

The victory is achieved under the banner of faith, and under no other banners; the striving is purely for the sake of God, for the success of His religion and His law, for the protection of **Dar-ul-Islam**, the particulars of which we have described above, and for no other purpose. It is not for the spoils or for fame, nor for the honor of a country or nation, nor for the mere protection of one's family except when supporting them against religious persecution.

The honor of martyrdom is achieved only when one is fighting in the cause of God, and if one is killed for any other purpose this honor will not be attained.

Any country which fights the Muslim because of his belief and prevents him from practicing his religion, and in which the **Shari'ah** is suspended, is Dar-ul-Harb, even though his family or his relatives or his people live in it, or his capital is invested and his trade or commerce is in that country; and any country where the Islamic faith is dominant and its **Shari'ah** is operative is **Dar-ul-Islam**, even though the Muslim's family or relatives or his people do not live there, and he does not have any commercial relations with it.

The fatherland is that place where the Islamic faith, the Islamic way of life, and the **Shari'ah** of God is dominant; only this meaning of 'fatherland' is worthy of the human being, Similarly, 'nationality' means belief and a way of life, and only this relationship is worthy of man's dignity.

Grouping according to family and tribe and nation, and race and color and country, are residues of the primitive state of man; these *jahili* groupings are from a period when man's spiritual values were at a low stage. The Prophet — peace be on him — has called them "dead things" against which man's spirit should revolt.

When the Jews claimed to be the chosen people of God on the basis of their race and nationality, God Most High rejected their claim and declared that in every period, in every ram and in every nation, there is only 'one criterion: that of faith.

وَقَالُوا كُونُوا هُودًا أَوْ نَصَارَىٰ تَهْتَدُوا ۗ قُلْ بَلْ مِلَّةَ إِبْرَاهِيمَ حَنِيفًا ۖ وَمَا كَانَ مِنَ
الْمُشْرِكِينَ ﴿١٣٥﴾ قُولُوا آمَنَّا بِاللَّهِ وَمَا أُنزِلَ إِلَيْنَا وَمَا أُنزِلَ إِلَىٰ إِبْرَاهِيمَ وَإِسْمَاعِيلَ
وَإِسْحَاقَ وَيَعْقُوبَ وَالْأَسْبَاطِ وَمَا أُوتِيَ مُوسَىٰ وَعِيسَىٰ وَمَا أُوتِيَ النَّبِيُّونَ مِن رَّبِّهِمْ ۚ
لَا نُفَرِّقُ بَيْنَ أَحَدٍ مِّنْهُمْ ۖ وَنَحْنُ لَهُ مُسْلِمُونَ ﴿١٣٦﴾ فَإِنْ آمَنُوا بِمِثْلِ مَا آمَنتُم بِهِ فَقَدِ
اهْتَدَوا ۖ وَّإِن تَوَلَّوْا فَإِنَّمَا هُمْ فِي شِقَاقٍ ۖ فَسَيَكْفِيكَهُمُ اللَّهُ ۚ وَهُوَ السَّمِيعُ الْعَلِيمُ ﴿١٣٧﴾
صِبْغَةَ اللَّهِ ۖ وَمَنْ أَحْسَنُ مِنَ اللَّهِ صِبْغَةً ۖ وَنَحْنُ لَهُ عَابِدُونَ ﴿١٣٨﴾

***"And they say: 'become Jews, or Christians; then you will be guided'. Say: 'Not so: The way of Abraham, the pure in faith; and he was not among those who associate other gods with God'. Say: 'We believe in God, and what has come down to***

> *us, and what has come down to Abraham, Ismail and Isaac and Jacob and the Tribes (of Israelites), and what was given to Moses and Jesus and to other Prophets by their Sustainer. We do not make any distinction among them, and we have submitted to Him. if then they believe as you have believed, they are guided; but if they turn away, then indeed they are stubborn. Then God suffices for you, and He is All — Hearing, All — Knowing. The baptism of God: and who can baptise better than God? And we worship Him alone."* (2:135-138)

The people who are really chosen by God are the Muslim community which has gathered under God's banner without regard to differences of races, nations, colors and countries.

كُنْتُمْ خَيْرَ أُمَّةٍ أُخْرِجَتْ لِلنَّاسِ تَأْمُرُونَ بِالْمَعْرُوفِ
وَتَنْهَوْنَ عَنِ الْمُنْكَرِ وَتُؤْمِنُونَ بِاللَّهِ

> *"You are the best community raised for the good of mankind. You enjoin what is good and forbid what is evil, and you believe in God."* (3:110)

This is that community in the first generation of which there were Abu Bakr from Arabia, Bilal from Abyssinia, Suhaib from Syria, Selman from Persia, and their brothers in faith. The generations which followed them were similar. Nationalism here is belief, homeland here is **Dar-ul-Islam**, the ruler here is God, and the constitution here is the Qur'an. This noble conception of homeland, of nationality, and of relationship should become imprinted on the hearts of those who invite others toward God. They should remove all influences of ***Jahiliyyah*** which make this concept impure and which may have the slightest element of hidden **Shirk**, such as **Shirk** in relation to homeland, or in relation to race or nation, or in relation to lineage or material interests. All these have been mentioned by God Most High in one verse, in which He has placed them in one side of the balance and the belief and its responsibilities in the other side, and invites people to choose.

قُلْ إِنْ كَانَ آبَاؤُكُمْ وَأَبْنَاؤُكُمْ وَإِخْوَانُكُمْ وَأَزْوَاجُكُمْ وَعَشِيرَتُكُمْ وَأَمْوَالٌ
اقْتَرَفْتُمُوهَا وَتِجَارَةٌ تَخْشَوْنَ كَسَادَهَا وَمَسَاكِنُ تَرْضَوْنَهَا أَحَبَّ إِلَيْكُمْ مِنَ اللَّهِ

وَرَسُوْلِهٖ وَجِهَادٍ فِيْ سَبِيْلِهٖ فَتَرَبَّصُوْا حَتّٰى يَاْتِيَ اللّٰهُ بِاَمْرِهٖ ۗ
وَاللّٰهُ لَا يَهْدِى الْقَوْمَ الْفٰسِقِيْنَ ۝

***"Say: If your fathers and your sons and your brothers and and your spouses and your relatives, and the wealth which you have acquired, and the commerce in which you fear decline, and the homes in which you take delight, are dearer to you than God and His Messenger and striving in His cause, then wait until God brings His judgment; and God does not guide the rebellious people."*** *(9:24)*

The callers to Islam should not have any superficial doubts in their hearts concerning the nature of ***Jahiliyyah*** and the nature of Islam, and the characteristics of **Dar-ul-Harb** and of **Dar-ul-Islam**, for through these doubts many are led to confusion. Indeed, there is no Islam in a land where Islam — is not dominant and where its **Shari'ah** is not established; and that place is not **Dar-ul-Islam** where Islam's way of life and its laws are not practiced. There is nothing beyond faith except unbelief, nothing beyond Islam except **Jahiliyyah**, nothing beyond the truth except falsehood.

## CHAPTER 10

# FAR — REACHING CHANGES

When we invite people to Islam, whether they are Believers or non — believers, we should keep in mind one fact, a fact which is a characteristic of Islam itself and which can be seen in its history. Islam is a comprehensive concept of life and the universe with its own unique characteristics. The concept of human life in all its aspects and relationships which are derived from it is also a complete system which has its particular characteristics. This concept is basically against all the new or old ***jahili*** concepts. Although there might be some details in which there are similarities between Islam and the ***jahili*** concepts, in relation to the principles from which these particulars are derived, the Islamic concept is different from all other theories with which man has been — familiar.

The first function of Islam is that it moulds human life according to this concept and gives it a practical form, and establishes a system in the world which has been prescribed by God; and for this very purpose God has raised this Muslim nation to be a practical example for mankind. God Most High says:

كُنْتُمْ خَيْرَ أُمَّةٍ أُخْرِجَتْ لِلنَّاسِ تَأْمُرُونَ بِالْمَعْرُوفِ
وَتَنْهَوْنَ عَنِ الْمُنْكَرِ وَتُؤْمِنُونَ بِاللَّهِ

***"You are the best community raised for the good of mankind. You enjoin what is good and forbid what is evil, and you believe in God".*** *(3:110)*

and He characterizes this community as follows:

الَّذِينَ إِنْ مَكَّنَّاهُمْ فِي الْأَرْضِ أَقَامُوا الصَّلَاةَ وَآتَوُا الزَّكَاةَ
وَأَمَرُوا بِالْمَعْرُوفِ وَنَهَوْا عَنِ الْمُنْكَرِ

> ***"Those who, if We give them authority in the land, establish regular prayers, pay Zakat, enjoin good, and forbid evil."*** *(22:41)*

* * *

It is not the function of Islam to compromise with the concepts of ***Jahiliyyah*** which are current in the world or to coexist in the same land together with a ***jahili*** system. This was not the case when it first appeared in the world, nor will it be today or in the future. ***Jahiliyyah***, to whatever period it belongs, is ***Jahiliyyah***; that is, deviation from the worship o. One God and the way of life prescribed by God. It derives its system and laws and regulations and habits and standards and values from a source other than God. On the other hand, Islam is submission to God, and its function is to invite people away from ***Jahiliyyah*** toward Islam.

***Jahiliyyah*** is the worship of some people by others; that is to say, some people become dominant and make laws for others, regardless of whether these laws are against God's injunctions and without caring for the use or misuse of their authority.

Islam, on the other hand, is people's worshipping God alone, and deriving concepts and beliefs, laws and regulations and values from the authority of God, and freeing themselves from servitude to God's servants. This is the very nature of Islam and the nature of its role on the earth. This point should be emphasized to anyone whomsoever we invite to Islam, whether they be Muslims or non — Muslims.

Islam cannot accept any mixing with ***Jahiliyyah***, either in its concept or in the modes of living which are derived from this concept. Either Islam will remain, or ***Jahiliyyah***: Islam cannot accept or agree to a situation which is half — Islam and half — ***Jahiliyyah***. In this respect Islam's stand is very clear. It says that the truth is one and cannot be divided; if it is not the truth, then it must be falsehood. The mixing and co — existence of the truth and falsehood is impossible. Command belongs to God, or otherwise to ***Jahiliyyah***; God's **Shari'ah** will prevail, or else people's desires.

وَأَنِ احْكُمْ بَيْنَهُمْ بِمَآ أَنْزَلَ اللّٰهُ وَلَا تَتَّبِعْ أَهْوَآءَهُمْ وَاحْذَرْهُمْ
أَنْ يَّفْتِنُوْكَ عَنْۢ بَعْضِ مَآ أَنْزَلَ اللّٰهُ إِلَيْكَ

> ***"And judge between them according to what God has revealed, and do not follow their opinions, and beware of them lest they confuse you in***

*matters which God has revealed to you."* *(5:49)*

فَلِذٰلِكَ فَادْعُ ۚ وَاسْتَقِمْ كَمَآ اُمِرْتَ ۚ وَلَا تَتَّبِعْ اَهْوَآءَهُمْ ۚ

*"Then invi te them to this, and remain firmly committed to what you have been commanded, and do not follow their desires."* *(42:15)*

فَاِنْ لَّمْ يَسْتَجِيْبُوْا لَكَ فَاعْلَمْ اَنَّمَا يَتَّبِعُوْنَ اَهْوَآءَهُمْ ؕ وَمَنْ اَضَلُّ مِمَّنِ اتَّبَعَ
هَوٰىهُ بِغَيْرِ هُدًى مِّنَ اللّٰهِ ؕ اِنَّ اللّٰهَ لَا يَهْدِى الْقَوْمَ الظّٰلِمِيْنَ ﴿٥٠﴾

*"And if they do not respond to you, then know that they are following their own opinions; and who can be more misguided than one who follows his own opinion against the guidance from God? Indeed, God does not guide the wicked people".* *(28:50)*

ثُمَّ جَعَلْنٰكَ عَلٰى شَرِيْعَةٍ مِّنَ الْاَمْرِ فَاتَّبِعْهَا وَلَا تَتَّبِعْ اَهْوَآءَ الَّذِيْنَ لَا يَعْلَمُوْنَ ﴿١٨﴾

*"We have set you on a way ordained (by God); then follow it, and do not follow the desires of those who have no knowledge.* *(45:18)*

اَفَحُكْمَ الْجَاهِلِيَّةِ يَبْغُوْنَ ؕ وَمَنْ اَحْسَنُ مِنَ اللّٰهِ حُكْمًا لِّقَوْمٍ يُّوْقِنُوْنَ ﴿٥٠﴾

*"Do they want a judgment from the Days of Ignorance? Yet who is better in judgment than God, for a people having sure faith?* *(5:50)*

These verses make it clear that there are only two ways, and no third possibility exists: either to submit to God and His Messenger — peace be on him — or else to follow ***jahiliyyah***. If the law given by God is not made the arbiter, then naturally one will deviate from it. After this clear and decisive injunction from God Most High there is no room for any controversy or excuse — making.

The foremost duty of Islam in this world is to depose ***Jahiliyyah*** from the leadership of man, and to take the leadership into its own hands and enforce the particular way of life which is its permanent feature. The purpose of this rightly guided leadership is the good and success of mankind, the good which proceeds from returning to the Creator and the' success which comes from being in harmony with the rest of the universe. The intention is to raise human beings to that high position which God has chosen for them and to free them from the slavery of desires. This purpose is explained by Raba' bin 'Amer, when he replied to the commander — inchief of the Persian army, Rustum. Rustum asked, "For what purpose have you come?" Raba'i answered, "God has sent us to bring anyone who wishes from servitude to men into the service of God alone, from the narrowness of this world into the vastness of this world and the Hereafter, from the tyranny of religions into the justice of Islam."

Islam did not come to support people's desires, which are expressed in their concepts, institutions, modes of living, and habits and traditions, whether they were prevalent at the advent of Islam or are prevalent now, both in the East and in the West. Islam does not sanction the rule of selfish desires. It has come to abolish all such concepts, laws, customs and traditions, and to replace them with a new concept of human life, to create a new world on the foundation of submission to the Creator. Sometimes it appears that some parts of Islam resemble some aspects of the life of people in ***Jahiliyyah***; but these aspects are not ***jahili*** nor are they from ***Jahiliyyah***. This apparent resemblance in some minor aspects is a mere coincidence; the roots of the two trees are entirely different. The tree of Islam has been sown and nurtured by the wisdom of God, while the tree of ***Jahiliyyah*** is the product of the soil of human desires.

وَالْبَلَدُ الطَّيِّبُ يَخْرُجُ نَبَاتُهُ بِإِذْنِ رَبِّهِ ۖ وَالَّذِي خَبُثَ لَا يَخْرُجُ إِلَّا نَكِدًا

***"The fertile piece of land grows good vegetation with the permission of its Lord, while the bad land brings forth but little."*** *(7:58)*

***Jahiliyyah*** is evil and corrupt, whether it be of the ancient or modern variety. Its outward manifestations may be different during different epochs, yet its roots are the same. Its roots are human desires, which do not let people come out of their ignorance and self — importance, desires which are used in the interests of some persons or some classes or some nations or some races, which interests prevail over the demand for justice, truth and goodness. But the pure law of God cuts through these roots and provides a system of laws which has no human interference, and it is not influenced by human ignorance or human desire or for the interests of a particular group of people.

This is the basic difference between the concept of life taught by God and man made theories, and hence it is impossible to gather them together under one system. It is fruitless to try to construct a system of life which is half — Islam and half — ***Jahiliyyah***. God does not forgive any association with His person, and He does not accept any association with His revealed way of life. Both are equally **Shirk** in the sight of God, as both are the product of the same mentality.

This truth ought to be firmly and clearly impressed on our minds, and when we present Islam to people our tongues should not hesitate to pronounce it, nor should we be ashamed, nor should we leave any doubt in people's minds, nor leave them until they are assured that if they follow Islam their lives will be completely changed. Islam will change their concepts of life as well as their modes of behaviour completely. As it changes them, it bestows on them blessings beyond imagination by uplifting their concepts, improving their modes of behaviour, and bringing them closer to the position of dignity worthy of human life. Nothing will remain of the modes of ***Jahiliyyah*** in which they were steeped, except some minor aspects which by accident appear similar to some aspects of Islam. Even these will not remain exactly the same as they become joined to the great root of Islam, which is clearly different from the root to which they had been joined so far, the fruitless and evil root of ***Jahiliyyah***. During this process it will not deprive them of any of the knowledge based on scientific observation; indeed, it gives a great impetus in this direction.

When we call people to Islam, it is our duty to make them understand that it is not one of the man — made religions or ideologies, nor is it a man — made system — with various names, banners and paraphernalia — but it is Islam, and nothing else. Islam has its own permanent personality and permanent concept and permanent modes. Islam guarantees for mankind a blessing greater than all these man — made systems. Islam is noble, pure, just, beautiful, springing from the source of the Most High, the Most Great God.

* * *

When we understand the essence of Islam in this manner, this understanding in itself creates in us confidence and power, compassion and sympathy, while presenting Islam to the people: the confidence of a man who knows that he is with the truth, while what the people have is falsehood; and the compassion of a person who sees the suffering of mankind and knows how to bring them to ease; and the sympathy of a person who sees the error of the people and knows what supreme guidance is.

We need not rationalize Islam to them, need not appease their desires and distorted concepts. We will be extremely outspoken with them: "The ignorance in which you are living makes you impure, and God wants to purify you; the customs which you follow are defiling, and God wants to cleanse you; the life you are living is low, and God wants to uplift you; the condition which you are in is troublesome, depressing and base, and God wants to give you ease, mercy and goodness. Islam will change your concepts, your modes of living and your values; will raise you to another life so that you will look upon the life you are now living with disgust; will show you modes of living such that you will look upon all other modes, whether Eastern or Western, with contempt; and will introduce you to values such that you will look upon all current values in the world with disdain. And if, because of the sorry state you are in, you cannot see the true picture of the Islamic life, since your enemies — the enemies of this religion — are all united against the establishment of this way of life, against its taking a practical form, then let us show it to you; and, thank God, its picture is in our hearts, seen through the windows of our Qur'an, of our **Shari'ah**, of our history, of our concept of the future, whose coming we do not doubt!"

* * *

This is the way in which we ought to address people while presenting Islam. This is the truth, and this was the form in which Islam addressed people for the first time; this was the form, whether it was in the Arabian peninsula, in Persia or in the Roman provinces, or in whatever other places it went.

Islam looked at them from a height, as this is its true position, and addressed them with extreme love and kindness, as this is its true temperament, and explained everything to them with complete clarity, without any ambiguity, as this is its method. It never said to them that it would not touch their way of living, their modes, their concepts and their values except perhaps slightly; it did not propose similarities with their system or manners to please them, as some do today when they present Islam to the people under the names of 'Islamic Democracy' or 'Islamic Socialism', or sometimes by saying that the current economic or political or legal systems in the world need not be changed except a little to be acceptable Islamically. The purpose of all this rationalization is to appease people's desires!

Indeed, the matter is entirely different! The change from this ***Jahiliyyah***, which has encompassed the earth, to Islam is vast and far — reaching; and the Islamic life is the opposite of all modes of ***jahili*** life, whether ancient or modern. The miserable state of mankind is not alleviated by a few minor changes in current systems and modes. Mankind will never come out of it without this vast and far — reaching change — the change from the ways of the created to the way of the Creator, from the systems of men to the system of the Lord of men, and from the commands of servants to the command of the Lord of 'servants.

This is a fact — a fact which we proclaim, and proclaim loudly, without leaving any doubt or ambiguity in the minds of people.

In the beginning, people may dislike this method of giving the message, may run away from it, and may be afraid of it. But the people disliked it, ran away from it, and were afraid of it, when Islam was presented to them for the first time. They hated it and were hurt when Muhammad — peace be on him — criticized their concepts, derided their deities, rejected their ways of behaviour, turned away from their habits and customs, and adopted for himself and for the few believers who were with him modes of behaviour, values and customs other than the modes, values and customs of ***Jahiliyyah***.

Then what happened? They loved the same truth which at first seemed so strange to them, from which they ran away

كَأَنَّهُمْ حُمُرٌ مُّسْتَنفِرَةٌ ﴿٥٠﴾ فَرَّتْ مِن قَسْوَرَةٍ ﴿٥١﴾

> ***"as if they were startled donkeys fleeing before a lion ..."*** *(74:50-51)*

against which they fought with all their power and strategy, grievously torturing its adherents when they were weak in Mecca and fighting with them incessantly when they were strong in Medina.

The conditions which the Islamic Call had to face in its first period were not more favourable or better than the conditions of today. It was an unknown thing, rejected by ***Jahiliyyah***; it was confined to the valley of Mecca, hounded by the people in power and authority; and, at that time, it was a complete stranger to the whole world. It was surrounded by mighty and proud empires which were against its basic teachings and purposes. In spite of all this it was a powerful Call, as it is powerful today and will remain powerful tomorrow. The source of its real power is hidden in the very nature of this belief; that is why it can operate under the worst conditions and in the face of the most severe opposition. It derives its power from the simple and clear truth on which it stands. Its balanced teachings are according to human nature — that nature which cannot tolerate any resistance for very long — and it is in its power to lead mankind over toward progress, no matter in what stage of economic, social, scientific or intellectual backwardness or development it may be. Another secret of its power is that it challenges ***Jahiliyyah*** and its physical power, without agreeing to change even a single letter of its principles. It does not compromise with ***jahili*** inclinations nor does it use rationalizations. It proclaims the truth boldly so that people may understand that it is good, that it is a mercy and a blessing.

It is God Who created men and Who knows their nature and the passages to their hearts. He knows how they accept the truth when it is proclaimed boldly, clearly, forcefully, and without hesitation and doubt!

Indeed, the capacity exists in human nature to change completely from one way of life to another; and this is much easier for it than many partial changes. And if the complete change were to be from one system of life to another which is higher, more perfect and purer than the former, this complete change is agreeable to human psychology. But who would be agreeable to changing from a system of ***Jahiliyyah*** to the system of Islam if the Islamic system were no more than a little change here and a little variation there? To continue with the former system is more logical. At least it is an established order, amenable to reform and change; then what is the need to abandon it for an order not yet established or applied, while it continues to resemble the old order in all its major characteristics?

* * *

We also find some people who, when talking about Islam, present it to the people as if it were something which is being accused and they want to defend it against the accusation. Among their defences, one goes like this: "It is said that modern systems have done such and such, while Islam did not do anything comparable. But listen! It did all this some fourteen hundred years before modern civilization!"

Woe to such a defence! Shame on such a defence!

Indeed, Islam does not take its justifications from the ***jahili*** system and its evil derivatives. And these 'civilizations', which have dazzled many and have defeated their spirits, are nothing but a ***jahili*** system at heart, and this system is erroneous, hollow and worthless in comparison with Islam. The argument that the people living under it are in a better condition than the people of a so — called Islamic country or "the Islamic world' has no weight. The people in these countries have reached this wretched state by abandoning Islam, and not because they are Muslims. The argument which Islam presents to people is this: Most certainly. Islam is better beyond imagination. It has come to change ***Jahiliyyah***, not to continue it; to elevate mankind from its depravity, and not to bless its manifestations which have taken the garb of 'civilization'.

We ought not to be defeated to such an extent that we start looking for similarities with Islam in the current systems or in some current religions or in some current ideas; we reject these systems in the East as well as in the West. We reject them all, as indeed they are retrogressive and in opposition to the direction toward which Islam intends to take mankind.

When we address people in this fashion and present to them the basic message of the comprehensive concept of Islam, the justification for changing from one concept to another, from one mode of living to another, will come from the very depths of their being. But we will not address them with this ineffective argument, saying: "Come from a system which is currently established to a system not yet applied; it will make only a little change in the established order. You should have no objection; you can continue to do what you have been doing. It will not bother you except to ask for a few changes in your habits, manners and inclinations, and will preserve for you whatever pleases you and will not touch it except very slightly."

On the surface this method seems easy, but there is no attraction in it; moreover, it is not based , on the truth. The truth is that Islam not only changes concepts and attitudes, but also the system and modes, laws and customs, since this change is so fundamental that no relationship can remain with the *jahili* way of life, the life which mankind is living. It is sufficient to say that it brings them both in general and in particular from servitude to men into the service of God, Who is One:

> ***"Believe if one wishes or reject if one wishes."***
>
> ***"And if one rejects, then God is independent of His creation,"***

The question in essence is that of unbelief and belief, of associating others with God and the Oneness of God, and of ***Jahiliyyah*** and Islam. This ought to be made clear. Indeed, people are not Muslims, as they proclaim to be, as long as they live the life of ***Jahiliyyah***. If someone wishes to deceive himself or to deceive others by believing that Islam can be brought in line with this ***Jahiliyyah***, it is up to him. But whether this deception is for others, it cannot change anything of the actual reality. This is not Islam, and they are not Muslims. Today the task of the Call is to return these ignorant people to Islam and make them into Muslims all over again.

We are not inviting people to Islam to obtain some reward from them; we do not desire anything at all for ourselves, nor is our accounting and reward with the people. Indeed, we invite people to Islam because we love them and we wish them well, although they may torture us; and this is the characteristic of the caller to Islam and this is his motivation. The people are entitled to learn from us the nature of Islam and the nature of the obligations it imposes on them, as well as the great blessing which it bestows on them. They are also entitled to know that the nature of what they are doing is nothing but ***Jahiliyyah***; it is indeed ***Jahiliyyah***, with nothing in it from Islam. It is mere desire as long as it is not the **Shari'ah**; and it is falsehood as long as it is not the truth — and what is beyond the truth but falsehood!

* * *

There is nothing in our Islam of which we are ashamed or anxious about defending; there is nothing in it to be smuggled to the people with deception, nor do we muffle the loud truth which it proclaims. This is the defeated mentality, defeated before the West and before the East and before this and that mode of ***Jahiliyyah***, which is found in some people — 'Muslims' — who search for resemblances to Islam in man — made systems, or who find justification for the actions of Islam and its decision concerning certain matters by means of the actions of ***jahili*** civilization.

A person who feels the need of defence, justification and apology is not capable of presenting Islam to people. Indeed, he is a person who lives the life of ***Jahiliyyah***, hollow and full of contradictions, defects and evils, and intends to provide justification for the ***Jahiliyyah*** he is in. These are the offenders against Islam and they distract some sincere persons. They confuse Islam's true nature by their defence, as if Islam were something accused standing at trial, anxious for its own defence.

During my stay in the United States, there were some people of this kind who used to argue with us — with us few who were considered to be on the side of Islam. Some of them took the position of defence and justification. I, on the other hand, took the position of attacking the Western ***Jahiliyyah***, its shaky religious beliefs, its social and economic modes, and its immoralities: "Look at these concepts of the Trinity, Original Sin, Sacrifice and Redemption, which are agreeable neither to reason nor to conscience. Look at this capitalism with its monopolies, its usury and whatever else is unjust in it; at this individual freedom, devoid of human sympathy and responsibility for relatives except under the force of law; at this materialistic attitude which deadens the spirit; at this behaviour, like animals, which you call 'Free mixing of the sexes; at this vulgarity which you call 'emancipation of women,' at these unfair and cumbersome laws of marriage and divorce, which are contrary to the demands of practical life; and at Islam, with its logic, beauty, humanity and happiness, which reaches the horizons to which man strives but does not reach. It is a practical way of life and its solutions are based on the foundation of the wholesome nature of man."

These were the realities of Western life which we encountered. These facts, when seen in the light of Islam, made the American people blush. Yet there are people — exponents of Islam — who are defeated before this filth in which ***Jahiliyyah*** is steeped, even to the extent that they search for resemblances to Islam among this rubbish heap of the West, and also among the evil and dirty materialism of the East.

* * *

After this, there is no need for me to say: Certainly we who present Islam to the people are not the ones to go along with any of the concepts, modes and traditions of ***Jahiliyyah*** however great its pressure on us may be.

Our first task is to replace this ***Jahiliyyah*** with Islamic ideas and traditions. This cannot be brought about by agreeing with ***Jahiliyyah*** and going along a few, steps with it from the very beginning, as some of us think we ought to do, for this will simply mean that from the very beginning we have accepted defeat.

Of course the current ideas of the society and its prevalent traditions apply great pressure — back — breaking pressure, especially in the case of women; the Muslim woman is really under extreme and oppressive pressure — but this is the situation and we have to face it. First we must be steadfast; next we must prevail upon it; then we must show ***Jahiliyyah*** the low state it is really in compared to the lofty and bright horizons of Islamic life which we wish to attain.

This cannot come about by going along a few steps with ***Jahiliyyah***, nor by now severing relations with it and removing ourselves to a separate corner; never. The correct procedure is to mix with discretion, give and take with dignity, speak the truth with love, and show the superiority of the Faith with humility. After all this, we must realize the fact that we live in the midst of ***Jahiliyyah***, that our way of life is straighter than that of ***Jahiliyyah***, and that the change from ***Jahiliyyah*** to Islam is vast and far — reaching. The chasm between Islam and ***Jahiliyyah*** is great, and a bridge is not to be built across it so that the people on the two sides may mix with each other, but only so that the people of ***Jahiliyyah*** may come over to Islam, whether they reside in a so — called Islamic country and consider themselves Muslims or they are outside the 'Islamic' country, in order that they may come out of darkness into light and may get rid of their miserable condition, and enjoy those blessings which we have tasted — we who have understood Islam and live in its atmosphere. If not, then we shall say to them what God commanded His Messenger — peace be on him — to say:

لَكُمْ دِينُكُمْ وَلِيَ دِينِ ۝٦

***"For you your way, for me mine."*** *(109:6)*

## CHAPTER 11

# THE FAITH TRIUMPHANT

وَلَا تَهِنُوا وَلَا تَحْزَنُوا وَأَنتُمُ الْأَعْلَوْنَ إِن كُنتُم مُّؤْمِنِينَ ﴿١٣٩﴾

***"Do not be dejected nor grieve. You shall be the uppermost if you are Believers."*** *(3:139)*

The first thought which comes to mind on reading this verse is that it relates to the form of **Jihaad** which is actual fighting; but the spirit of this message and it application, with its manifold implications, is greater and wider than this particular aspect. Indeed, it describes that eternal state of mind which ought to inspire the Believer's consciousness, his thoughts, his estimates of things, events, values and persons.

It describes a triumphant state which should remain fixed in the Believer's heart in the face of every thing, every condition, every standard and every person; the superiority of the Faith and its value above all values which are derived from a source other than the source of the Faith.

It means to be above all the powers of the earth which have deviated from the way of the Faith, above all the values of the earth not derived from the source of the Faith, above all the customs of the earth not coloured with the colouring of the Faith, above all the laws of the laws of the earth not sanctioned by the Faith, and above all traditions not originating in the Faith.

It means to feel superior to others when weak, few and poor, as well as when strong, many and rich.

It means the sense of supremacy which does not give in before any rebellious force, before any social custom and erroneous tradition, before any behaviour which may be popular among people but which has no authority in the Faith. Steadfastness and strength on the battlefield — are but one expression among many of the triumphant spirit which is included in this statement of Almighty God.

* * *

The superiority through faith is not a mere single act of will nor a passing euphoria nor a momentary passion, but is a sense of superiority based on the permanent truth centered in the very nature of existence. This eternal truth is above the logic of force, the concept of environment, the terminology of society, and the customs of people, as indeed it is joined with the Living God Who does not die.

A society has a governing logic and a common mode, its pressure is strong and its weight heavy on anyone who is not protected by some powerful member of the society or who challenges it without a strong force. Accepted concepts and current ideas have a climate of their own, and it is difficult to get rid of them without a deep sense of truth, in the light of which all these concepts and ideas shrink to nothingness, and without the help of a source which is superior, greater and stronger than the source of these concepts and ideas.

The person who takes a stand against the direction of the society — its governing logic, its common mode, its values and standards, its ideas and concepts, its error and deviations — will find himself a stranger, as well as helpless, unless his authority comes from a source which is more powerful than the people, more permanent than the earth, and nobler than life.

Indeed, God does not leave the Believer alone in the face of oppression to whimper under its weight, to suffer dejection and grief, but relieves him of all this with the message:

وَلَا تَهِنُوا وَلَا تَحْزَنُوا وَأَنتُمُ الْأَعْلَوْنَ إِن كُنتُم مُّؤْمِنِينَ ﴿١٣٩﴾

***"Do not be dejected nor grieve; you shall be the uppermost if you are Believers."*** *(3:139)*

This message relieves him from both dejection and grief, these two feelings being natural for a human being in this situation. It relieves him of both, not merely through patience and steadfastness, but also through a sense of superiority from whose heights the power of oppression, the dominant values, the current concepts, the standards, the rules, the customs and habits, and the people steeped in error, all seem low.

Indeed, the Believer is uppermost — uppermost on the basis of the authority which is behind him and his source of guidance. Then, what is to be said of this earth, what of the people, what of the dominant values of the world, the standards current among people, while he is inspired by God, returns to God for guidance, and travels on His path?

The Believer is most superior in his understanding and his concept of the nature of the world, for the belief in One God, in the form which has come to him from Islam, is the most perfect form of understanding, the greatest truth. The picture of the world which this Faith presents is far above the heaps of concepts, beliefs and religions, and is not reached by any great philosophers, ancient or modern, nor attained by idolaters or the followers of distorted scriptures, nor approached by the base materialists. This picture is so bright, clear, beautiful and balanced that the glory of the Islamic belief shines forth as never before. And without doubt those who have grasped this knowledge are superior to all others.[20]

The Believer is most superior in his values and standards, by means of which he measures life, events, things, and persons. The source of his belief is the knowledge of God and His attributes as described by Islam, and the knowledge of the realities prevalent in the universe at large, not merely on the small earth. This belief with its grandeur provides the Believer with values which are superior to and firmer than the defective standards made by men, who do not know anything except what is under their feet. They do not agree on the same standard within the same generation; even the same person changes his standard from moment to moment.

He is most superior in his conscience and understanding, in his morals and manners, as he believes in God Who has excellent names and attributes. This by itself creates in him a sense of dignity, purity and cleanliness, modesty and piety, and a desire for good deeds, and of being a rightly — guided representative of God on earth. Furthermore, this belief gives him the assurance that the reward is in the Hereafter, the reward before which the troubles of the world and all its sorrows become insignificant. The heart of the Believer is content with it, although he may pass through, this life without apparent success.

And he is most superior in his law and system of life. When the Believer scans whatever man, ancient or modern, has known, and compares it with his own law and system, he realizes that all this is like the playthings of children or the searchings of blind men in comparison with the përfect system and the complete law of Islam. And when he looks from his height at erring mankind with compassion and sympathy at its helplessness and error, he finds nothing in his heart except a sense of triumph over error and nonsense.

* * *

This was the attitude of the early Muslims toward the hollow expressions of pomp and power and the traditions which had enslaved the people of

20. See the chapter "Teeh wa rukam." in the book, **"Khasais al-Tasawwar al-Islami wa Muqawwimatuhu"**, by the author.

the Days of Ignorance. Ignorance is not limited to any particular age, but is a condition which reappears whenever people deviate from the way of Islam, whether in the past, present or future.

This was the response of al-Mughira ibn Sh'uba when he encountered the forms, manners, standards, and expressions of ***Jahiliyyah*** in the camp of Rustum, the famous Persian general.

"Abi Uthman al-Nahdi reports: When al-Mughira crossed the bridge and reached the Persian army, they seated him and asked Rustum's permission for an audience. In spite of their defeat, they had not changed any of their show of pomp. Al-Mughira proceeded. The people were all in their military uniforms, many wearing crowns, and clothed in gold — threaded garments. The floor was thickly carpeted (the carpet extending to three hundred or four hundred steps) and was to be traversed to reach the general. Al-Mughira proceeded, his hair braided in four braids, and climbed on the throne and sat beside Rustum. The attendants jumped on him and pulled him down. He then said, 'We had heard that you were a sensible people, but I see that you are the most foolish nation. Among Arabs all are equal and no one is slave to another, except when one is captured on the battlefield. I imagined that you treated each other equally as we do. It would have been better if you had informed me that some of you are lords over others rather than treating me like this. This is not good manners, and we do not do it. I have come at your request and not on my own. I know now that your situation is weak and that you will be defeated. No kingdom can survive with this character and mentality."

A similar attitude was shown by Raba'i bin 'Amer in front of Rustum and his courtiers before the battle of al-Qadisyyah:

"Before the battle of al-Qadisyyah, S' ad bin Waqqas sent Raba'i bin 'Amer as a messenger to Rustum, the commander of the Persian army and their ruler. He entered the tent, which was all carpeted and curtained with silk and velvet. Rustum sat on a golden throne, crowned and wearing precious stones and pearls. Raba'i, in tattered clothes, with a shield, sitting on a small horse, entered. He did not alight from his horse for some distance; then he alighted and tied the horse to — alarge pillow. He proceeded armed and helmeted. They said to him: 'Take off your arms'. He replied: 'I have not come on my own but on your request. If you do not like it, then I will go back'. Rustum said: 'Let him come'. He came forward leaning on his spear, making holes in the carpet. Rustum asked him: 'For what purpose you have come?" He replied: 'God has sent us to bring whoever wishes from servitude to men into the service of God alone, from the narrowness of this world into the vastness of this world and the Hereafter, from the tyranny of religions into the justice of Islam".

(Ibn Kathir: Al-Bidayahwa al-Nihayah)

* * *

Conditions change, the Muslim loses his physical power and is conquered; yet the consciousness does not depart from him that he is the most superior. If he remains a Believer, he looks upon his conqueror from a superior position. He remains certain that this is a temporary condition which will pass away and that faith will turn the tide from which there is no escape. Even if death is his portion, he will never bow his head. Death comes to all, but for him there is martyrdom. He will proceed to the Garden, while his conquerors go to the Fire. What a difference! And he hears the voice of his Generous Lord:

لَا يَغُرَّنَّكَ تَقَلُّبُ الَّذِينَ كَفَرُوا فِي الْبِلَادِ ﴿١٩٦﴾ مَتَاعٌ قَلِيلٌ ثُمَّ مَأْوَاهُمْ جَهَنَّمُ ۚ
وَبِئْسَ الْمِهَادُ ﴿١٩٧﴾ لَٰكِنِ الَّذِينَ اتَّقَوْا رَبَّهُمْ لَهُمْ جَنَّاتٌ تَجْرِي مِن تَحْتِهَا الْأَنْهَارُ
خَالِدِينَ فِيهَا نُزُلًا مِّنْ عِندِ اللَّهِ ۗ وَمَا عِندَ اللَّهِ خَيْرٌ لِّلْأَبْرَارِ ﴿١٩٨﴾

***"Let it not deceive you that the unbelievers walk about in the land. A little respite and their abode is Hell, and what an evil place! But for those who fear their Lord are Gardens through which rivers flow, to abide therein — a hospitality from God; and that which is with God is best for the righteous."*** ***(3:196-198)***

The society may be drowned in lusts, steeped in low passions, rolling in filth and dirt, thinking that it has 'enjoyment and freedom from chains and restrictions. Such a society may become devoid of any clean enjoyment and even of lawful food, and nothing may remain except a rubbish heap, or dirt and mud. The Believer from his height looks at the people drowning in dirt and mud. He may be the only one; yet he is not dejected nor grieved, nor does his heart desire that he take off his neat and immaculate garments and join the crowd. He remains the uppermost with the enjoyment of faith and the taste of belief.

The believer holds on to his religion like the holder of a precious stone in the society deyoid of religion, of character, of high values, of noble manners and of whatever is clean, pure and beautiful. The others mock his tenacity, ridicule his ideas, laugh at his values, but this does not make the Believer weak of heart: and he looks from his height at those who mock, ridicule and laugh, and he says, as one of the great souls — those who preceded him on the long and bright path of faith, Noah (peace be on him), said:

إِن تَسْخَرُوا مِنَّا فَإِنَّا نَسْخَرُ مِنكُمْ كَمَا تَسْخَرُونَ ﴿٣٨﴾

> ***"You ridicule us! Yet indeed we shall ridicule you as you ridicule."*** *(11:38)*

And he sees the end of this bright path, and also the end of the dark path in the words of God:

إِنَّ الَّذِينَ أَجْرَمُوا كَانُوا مِنَ الَّذِينَ آمَنُوا يَضْحَكُونَ ﴿٢٩﴾ وَإِذَا مَرُّوا بِهِمْ يَتَغَامَزُونَ ﴿٣٠﴾
وَإِذَا انقَلَبُوا إِلَىٰ أَهْلِهِمُ انقَلَبُوا فَكِهِينَ ﴿٣١﴾ وَإِذَا رَأَوْهُمْ قَالُوا إِنَّ هَٰؤُلَاءِ لَضَالُّونَ ﴿٣٢﴾
وَمَا أُرْسِلُوا عَلَيْهِمْ حَافِظِينَ ﴿٣٣﴾ فَالْيَوْمَ الَّذِينَ آمَنُوا مِنَ الْكُفَّارِ يَضْحَكُونَ ﴿٣٤﴾ عَلَى
الْأَرَائِكِ يَنظُرُونَ ﴿٣٥﴾ هَلْ ثُوِّبَ الْكُفَّارُ مَا كَانُوا يَفْعَلُونَ ﴿٣٦﴾

> ***"The criminals used to laugh at the Believers, wink at them in passing, and joke about them when they returned to their families. When they — saw them, they used to say: "Certainly these people are astray". Yet they were not sent as watchers over them. Today the Believers laugh at the unbelievers, and watch them while sitting on couches. Did the unbelievers' get their reward according to what they used to do"?*** *(83:29-36)*

Before this, the Holy Qur'an told us what the unbelievers said to the Believers:

وَإِذَا تُتْلَىٰ عَلَيْهِمْ آيَاتُنَا بَيِّنَاتٍ قَالَ الَّذِينَ كَفَرُوا لِلَّذِينَ آمَنُوا
أَيُّ الْفَرِيقَيْنِ خَيْرٌ مَّقَامًا وَأَحْسَنُ نَدِيًّا ﴿٧٣﴾

> ***"When Our clear verses are recited to them, the unbelievers say to the Believers: 'Which of the two parties is superior in station, better in assembly?"*** *(19:73)*

Which of the two parties? The great men who do not believe in Muhammad, or the poor who assemble around him? Which of the two parties? Al-Nadr bin al-Harith and 'Amr bin Hisham and al-Walid bin al-Mughira and Abu Sufyan bin Harb? Or Bilal and 'Ammar and Khabbab? If the call of Muhammad had been better, would only such people have followed him who did not have any power or position among the Quraish, who assembled in such a lowly place as the house of al-Arqam, while their opponents were the lords of al-Nadwah, the great and glorious assembly hall, and they possessed power, authority and grandeur?

This is the logic of this world, the logic of those of any age or any place who cannot see the higher horizons. It is the wisdom of God that belief remains independent of the glitter and glamour of wordly allurements, such as closeness to the ruler, favor from the government, popularity among the people or the satisfaction of desire. It is only striving, hard work, fighting and martydom. Let him accept it who may accept, who has the certainty in his heart that this is purely for the sake of God and not for the sake of people, or for the allurements and attractions so dear to people. Let him stay away from it who desires pleasures and benefits, and who is greedy for pomp and show, and who is after wealth and possessions, and who gives weight to the considerations of men although these may be light in the balance of God.

Indeed, the Believer does not borrow his values, concepts and standards from people so that he is dependent on the estimation of people; he takes them from the Sustainer of the people, and that is sufficient for him. He does not follow the desires of men so that he has to fluctuate with their changing desires; he depends on the firm balance of the truth which does not fluctuate or lean to one side. Indeed, his inspiration does not come from this passing and finite world; the inspiration of his soul comes from the fountainheads of the universe. Then how can he find dejection in his soul or grief in his heart, while he is linked to the Sustainer of the people, the balance of truth, and the fountainheads of the universe?

Indeed, he is with the truth — and what is beyond the truth but falsehood? Let falsehood have power, let it have its drums and banners, and let it have its throngs and mobs; all this cannot change anything of the truth. Indeed, he is with the truth, and nothing is beyond the truth except error, and the Believer cannot prefer error to the truth. He is a Believer, and whatever be the conditions and the situation, he cannot exchange error for the truth.

رَبَّنَا لَا تُزِغْ قُلُوبَنَا بَعْدَ إِذْ هَدَيْتَنَا وَهَبْ لَنَا مِن لَّدُنكَ رَحْمَةً ۚ إِنَّكَ أَنتَ
الْوَهَّابُ ﴿٨﴾ رَبَّنَا إِنَّكَ جَامِعُ النَّاسِ لِيَوْمٍ لَّا رَيْبَ فِيهِ ۚ إِنَّ اللَّهَ لَا يُخْلِفُ الْمِيعَادَ ﴿٩﴾

***"Our Master! Do not let our hearts waver after You have guided us, and bestow on us mercy from Yourself; indeed You are the Bestower. Our Master! You will gather mankind on the Day about which there is no doubt; indeed God does not fail in His promise."*** *(3:8-9)*

## CHAPTER 12

# THIS IS THE ROAD

وَ السَّمَآءِ ذَاتِ الْبُرُوْجِ ﴿١﴾ وَ الْيَوْمِ الْمَوْعُوْدِ ﴿٢﴾ وَ شَاهِدٍ وَّ مَشْهُوْدٍ ﴿٣﴾ قُتِلَ اَصْحٰبُ
الْاُخْدُوْدِ ﴿٤﴾ النَّارِ ذَاتِ الْوَقُوْدِ ﴿٥﴾ اِذْ هُمْ عَلَيْهَا قُعُوْدٌ ﴿٦﴾ وَّ هُمْ عَلٰى مَا يَفْعَلُوْنَ
بِالْمُؤْمِنِيْنَ شُهُوْدٌ ﴿٧﴾ وَ مَا نَقَمُوْا مِنْهُمْ اِلَّآ اَنْ يُّؤْمِنُوْا بِاللّٰهِ الْعَزِيْزِ الْحَمِيْدِ ﴿٨﴾
الَّذِيْ لَهٗ مُلْكُ السَّمٰوٰتِ وَ الْاَرْضِ ؕ وَ اللّٰهُ عَلٰى كُلِّ شَيْءٍ شَهِيْدٌ ﴿٩﴾ اِنَّ الَّذِيْنَ فَتَنُوا
الْمُؤْمِنِيْنَ وَ الْمُؤْمِنٰتِ ثُمَّ لَمْ يَتُوْبُوْا فَلَهُمْ عَذَابُ جَهَنَّمَ وَ لَهُمْ عَذَابُ الْحَرِيْقِ ﴿١٠﴾
اِنَّ الَّذِيْنَ اٰمَنُوْا وَ عَمِلُوا الصّٰلِحٰتِ لَهُمْ جَنّٰتٌ تَجْرِيْ مِنْ تَحْتِهَا الْاَنْهٰرُ ؕ ذٰلِكَ الْفَوْزُ
الْكَبِيْرُ ﴿١١﴾ اِنَّ بَطْشَ رَبِّكَ لَشَدِيْدٌ ﴿١٢﴾ اِنَّهٗ هُوَ يُبْدِئُ وَ يُعِيْدُ ﴿١٣﴾ وَ هُوَ الْغَفُوْرُ الْوَدُوْدُ ﴿١٤﴾
ذُو الْعَرْشِ الْمَجِيْدُ ﴿١٥﴾ فَعَّالٌ لِّمَا يُرِيْدُ ﴿١٦﴾

*"By the heavens with constellations; by the Promised Day; by the witness and the witnessed; doomed were the makers of the pit, abundantly supplied with fuel, as they sat by it and watched what they did with the Believers. They were outraged with them only because they believed in God, the All — Powerful, the All — Praiseworthy, He to Whom belongs the dominion of the heaven and the earth. And God is Witness over everything.*

*"Indeed, for those who persecute the believing men and women, and later do not repent, is the penalty of Hell; for them is the penalty of burning. As for those who believe and do good deeds, there are Gardens through which rivers flow, and*

> ***that is the great triumph. "Most certainly, strong is the grip of your Lord. It is He Who originates and repeats. And He is the Forgiving, the Loving, the Lord of the Throne, Performer of what He desires."*** *(85:1—16)*

The story of the Makers of the Pit as told in the chapter **"Al-Buruj"** ("The Constellations") requires deep thought by those among the Believers, to whatever time and place they belong, who invite people to God. The story, with its introduction, description, comments and moral, as related in the Qur'an, points out some profound truths concerning the nature of the Call toward God, the reaction of people to this Call, and the consequences which are possible in the vast scope of this Call — the scope whose vastness encompasses the whole world, this life and the life beyond it. The Qur'an through this story, points out to the Believers the road which lies before them and prepares them to accept with fortitude whatever comes their way, as yet unknown to them, with the permission of the All — Wise God.

This is the story of a group of people who believed in God and openly proclaimed their belief. They encountered tyrannical and oppressive enemies who were bent upon denying the right of a human being to believe in the All — Mighty, the All — Praiseworthy God. They intended to deprive man of that dignity which has been bestowed upon him by God and without which he is reduced to a mere plaything in the hands of tyrants, to be tortured, burned alive, and provide entertainment to his tormentors by his cries of agony.

But the faith in the hearts of the Believers raised them above all persecution. Belief triumphed over life. The threat of torture did not shake them, they never recanted, and they burned in the fire until death.

Indeed, their hearts were liberated from the worship of this life. Neither the love of life nor the fear of an agonizing death could make them yield to accept dishonor. They freed themselves from this earth and all its attractions, triumphing over life through a sublime faith.

Against these believing, righteous, sublime and honourable souls were pitted arrogant, mischievous, criminal and degraded people. And these criminals sat by the pit of fire, watching how the Believers suffered and writhed in pain. They sat there to enjoy the sight of how fire consumes living beings and how the bodies of these noble souls were reduced to cinders and ashes. And when some young man or woman, some child or old man from among these righteous Believers was thrown into the fire, their diabolical pleasure would reach a new height, and shouts of mad joy would escape their lips at the sight of blood and pieces of flesh.

This hair — raising incident shows that these rebellious people had sunk to those levels of depravity, seeking pleasure through torturing others, which are not even reached by any wild beast. A wild beast kills its prey for food, never to derive pleasure through tormenting it.

The same incident also shows the height to which the spirit of a Believer can soar, liberated and free — that height, the attainment of which has been the highest honor in all generations and in all periods.

By earthly reckoning, tyranny triumphed over faith, and this faith, although it reached its zenith in the hearts of this righteous, noble, steadfast and sublime group, had no weight in the struggle between tyranny and faith.

The traditions relating to this incident, like the text of the Qur'an, say nothing concerning whether God punished these tyrants in this life for their crimes as He punished the people, of Noah, the people of Hud, the people of Salih, the people of Sh'uaib, and the people of Lot, or as He caught Pharaoh with his army in all his splendor and power.

Thus from the earthly point of view, the end was pitiful and tragic.

But did this matter finish here? Did the group of Believers, with all the sublimity of their faith, vanish — vanish in the pit of fire with their torments? And did the group of criminals, with all the depravity of their crime, go unpunished?

From the earthly point of view, this tragic end troubles the heart! But the Qur'an teaches the Believers something else, reveals to them another reality, shows them another scale with which to weigh all matters, and enlightens them concerning the scope of the struggle.

Life's pleasures and pains, achievements and frustrations, do not have any great weight in the scale, and do not determine the profit or loss. Triumph is not limited to immediate victory, which is but one of the many forms of triumph.

In the scale of God, the true weight is the weight of faith; in God's market the only commodity in demand is the commodity of faith. The highest form of triumph is the victory of soul over matter, the victory of belief over pain, and the victory of faith over persecution. In the incident described above, the souls of the Believers were victorious over fear and pain, over the allurements of the earth and of life, and they gained such victory over torture which is an honor for all mankind for all times — and this is the true victory.

All men die, and of various causes; but not all gain such victory, nor reach such heights, nor taste such freedom, nor soar to such limits of the horizon. It is God's choosing and honouring a group of people who share death with the rest of mankind but who are singled out from other people for honour — honour among the noblest angels, nay, even among all man — kind, if we measure , them by the standards of the total history of generations of men.

It was possible for these Believers to save their lives by giving up their faith; but with how much loss to themselves, and with what a great loss to all mankind? They would have lost and would have killed this great truth, that life without belief is worthless, without freedom is degrading, and if tyrants are allowed to dominate men's souls as well as their bodies, then it is entirely depraved.

This was that noble truth, the great truth, which the Believers realized while they were alive on the earth; they realized and found it while the fire was licking them and burning their mortal frames. This noble truth triumphed over the torment of the fire.

The scope of this struggle is not limited to this earth or to this life. The observers of this struggle are not merely a generation of men. The angels are also participants in the happenings on earth; they observe them and are a witness to them, and they weigh them in a scale which is other than the scale of a generation or even of all generations of men. The angels are noble souls who number many times more than the people on the earth. Without question the praise and respect of the angels is far greater in this scale than the opinion and judgment of the people on the earth.

And then there is the Hereafter. That will be the real sphere which is adjacent to the earthly sphere and is not separated from it, in actuality as well as in the believers' perception of this reality. Thus the struggle does not end here, and the real decision cannot be reached here. Any judgment based on that part of it. which took place on earth is therefore incorrect, as this judgment will concern only a small and rather insignificant part of this struggle.

* * *

The former viewpoint, that is, that 'of the earthly scale, is limited and narrow, entertained by a hasty man. The latter viewpoint is comprehensive and far — sighted, and such a viewpoint is nurtured in a believer by the teachings of the Qur'an, as it is the mirror of reality and the basis of correct belief.

Among the rewards which God has promised to the Believers for their faith, obedience, steadfastness in the face of calamity, and victory over persecution is contentment of heart:

الَّذِينَ آمَنُوا وَتَطْمَئِنُّ قُلُوبُهُم بِذِكْرِ اللَّهِ ۗ أَلَا بِذِكْرِ اللَّهِ تَطْمَئِنُّ الْقُلُوبُ ٢٨

***"Those who believe, and their hearts find satisfaction in remembrance of God. Indeed, remembrance of God brings contentment to the hearts".*** *(13:28)*

And it is the pleasure and love of the All — Merciful:

إِنَّ الَّذِينَ آمَنُوا وَعَمِلُوا الصَّالِحَاتِ سَيَجْعَلُ لَهُمُ الرَّحْمَٰنُ وُدًّا ٩٦

***"Surely upon those who believe and do good deeds the All — Merciful shall assign love."***

*(19:96)*

And it is remembrance on High:

The Messenger of God — peace be on him — said: "When a certain person's child dies, God asks the angels: Did you take away the soul of My servant's child? They say: yes. Then He says: Did you take away the apple of his eye? They say Yes. Then He says: What did My servant say? They say: He praised You and said, 'Indeed, we belong to God and to Him shall we return'. Then He says: Build a house for My servant in the Garden and call it 'The House of Praise." (Tirmidhi)

He also said: "God Most High says: I am to My servant according to his thought concerning Me; when he remembers Me, I am with him; when he remembers Me to himself, I remember him to. Myself; when he mentions Me among a group, I mention him in a better group. If he comes toward Me one span, I come toward him an arm's length; if he comes toward Me one arm's length, I come toward him one step; if he walks toward Me, I run toward him." (Bukhari and Muslim)

And it is the keen interest of the angels in the affairs of the Believers on earth:

الَّذِينَ يَحْمِلُونَ الْعَرْشَ وَمَنْ حَوْلَهُ يُسَبِّحُونَ بِحَمْدِ رَبِّهِمْ وَيُؤْمِنُونَ بِهِ
وَيَسْتَغْفِرُونَ لِلَّذِينَ آمَنُوا ۖ رَبَّنَا وَسِعْتَ كُلَّ شَيْءٍ رَّحْمَةً وَعِلْمًا فَاغْفِرْ
لِلَّذِينَ تَابُوا وَاتَّبَعُوا سَبِيلَكَ وَقِهِمْ عَذَابَ الْجَحِيمِ ٧

***"The bearers of the Throne and those around it engage in their Lord's praise, and they believe***

> *in Him, and ask forgiveness for the Believers: 'Our Lord! Your mercy and knowledge encompass everything. Then forgive those who repent and follow Your path, and save them from the torment of Hell."* *(40:7)*

And it is life from God for the martyrs:

وَلَا تَحْسَبَنَّ الَّذِينَ قُتِلُوا فِي سَبِيلِ اللَّهِ أَمْوَاتًا ۚ بَلْ أَحْيَاءٌ عِنْدَ رَبِّهِمْ يُرْزَقُونَ ﴿١٦٩﴾
فَرِحِينَ بِمَا آتَاهُمُ اللَّهُ مِنْ فَضْلِهِ وَيَسْتَبْشِرُونَ بِالَّذِينَ لَمْ يَلْحَقُوا بِهِمْ مِنْ
خَلْفِهِمْ أَلَّا خَوْفٌ عَلَيْهِمْ وَلَا هُمْ يَحْزَنُونَ ﴿١٧٠﴾ يَسْتَبْشِرُونَ بِنِعْمَةٍ مِنَ اللَّهِ
وَفَضْلٍ وَأَنَّ اللَّهَ لَا يُضِيعُ أَجْرَ الْمُؤْمِنِينَ ﴿١٧١﴾

> *"Do not consider those as dead who were killed in the way of God; they are living and find sustenance from their Sustainer. They enjoy what God has given them from His bounty, and are glad for those who are left behind (on earth) and have not reached there yet, that they shall have no fear nor shall they grieve. They are jubilant at the favor from God and His bounty; indeed, God does not destroy the reward of the Believers".* *(3:169-171)*

And as to rejectors of faith, the tyrants and the criminals, God has repeatedly promised that He will catch them in the Hereafter, while giving them a limited period of living on earth: although He has caught some of them in this world too, yet for the final punishment emphasis is on the Hereafter:

لَا يَغُرَّنَّكَ تَقَلُّبُ الَّذِينَ كَفَرُوا فِي الْبِلَادِ ﴿١٩٦﴾ مَتَاعٌ قَلِيلٌ
ثُمَّ مَأْوَاهُمْ جَهَنَّمُ ۚ وَبِئْسَ الْمِهَادُ ﴿١٩٧﴾

> *"Do not let yourself be deceived that the unbelievers walk about in the land; a limited enjoyment, and then their abode is Hell, and what an evil place!"* *(3:196-197)*

وَلَا تَحْسَبَنَّ اللَّهَ غَافِلًا عَمَّا يَعْمَلُ الظَّالِمُونَ ۚ إِنَّمَا يُؤَخِّرُهُمْ لِيَوْمٍ
تَشْخَصُ فِيهِ الْأَبْصَارُ ﴿٤٢﴾ مُهْطِعِينَ مُقْنِعِي رُءُوسِهِمْ لَا يَرْتَدُّ إِلَيْهِمْ
طَرْفُهُمْ ۖ وَأَفْئِدَتُهُمْ هَوَاءٌ ﴿٤٣﴾

> ***"Do not think that God is unaware of the doings of the wicked people. He has deferred (judgement for) them to the Day when the eyes shall stare, and they shall run with necks outstretched and heads erect, their sight never returned to themselves, their hearts void".***
>
> *(14:42-43)*

فَذَرْهُمْ يَخُوضُوا وَيَلْعَبُوا حَتَّىٰ يُلَاقُوا يَوْمَهُمُ الَّذِي يُوعَدُونَ ﴿٤٢﴾ يَوْمَ يَخْرُجُونَ
مِنَ الْأَجْدَاثِ سِرَاعًا كَأَنَّهُمْ إِلَىٰ نُصُبٍ يُوفِضُونَ ﴿٤٣﴾ خَاشِعَةً أَبْصَارُهُمْ تَرْهَقُهُمْ
ذِلَّةٌ ۚ ذَٰلِكَ الْيَوْمُ الَّذِي كَانُوا يُوعَدُونَ ﴿٤٤﴾

> ***"Leave them to fun and play until the Day comes which they have been promised. On that Day they will come out of the graves and run as if hastening toward a fixed goal — eyes downcast, faces degraded. It will be the Day which they were promised".*** *(70:42-44)*

Thus the life of mankind is adjoined with that of the angels; this life proceeds into the life Hereafter; and the field of struggle between good and evil, between the truth and falsehood, and between faith and tyranny, is not limited to this earth. This matter does not finish here, nor is the decision made in this world. This life and all its pleasures and Tains, achievements and frustrations, do not weigh much in the scale.

The field of struggle is very broad in space and in time, in measures and in scales. This realization enlarges the Believer's horizons and heightens his aspirations, so that this earth and whatever is in it, this life and its attachments, shrink in his sight. The Believer's greatness increases in proportion to what he sees and understands of the scopes and horizons. To create such a broad, comprehensive, noble and pure concept of faith, the story of the Makers of the Pit is a great example.

* * *

Light is also thrown on another aspect of the Call toward God and its situation with respect to all possibilities in the story of the Makers of the Pit and the chapter "Constellations". ("al-Buruj")

The history of the Call toward God has witnessed various endings in this world in its struggle with other movements.

It has witnessed the annihilation of the people of Noah, the people of Hud, the people of Sh'uaib, and the people of Lot, and the escape — the bare escape — of a small group of believers. But the Qur'an does not state what these escapees did in the world and life after their escape. These examples tell us that sometimes God Most High gives the rebels and tyrants a taste of punishment in this world, while the full punishment still awaits them in the Hereafter.

This history of the Call witnessed the annihilation of Pharoah and his army, and the escape of Moses and his people and the establishment of their authority in the land. Those people of that time were the most righteous in all their (the Israelites') history, although they did not attain complete steadfastness nor establish the religion of God on earth in its entirety; and this example is different from the previous ones.

This history of the Call witnessed the annihilation of the polytheists who turned away from the guidance and belief in Muhammad — peace be on him — and it witnessed the complete victory of the Believers, with the amazing victory of belief in their hearts. And for the first time in the history of mankind the way, of God was established in such completeness as was not seen by man, either before or after.

And it witnessed, as we have seen, the example of the Makers of the Pit.

And it witnessed many other examples in earlier or later times with little mention in the history of faith. And even today it is witnessing such examples, which reach one or another of the possible endings recorded throughout history for centuries.

Among the various earlier or later examples, the example of the Makers of the Pit must not be forgotten.

The example must not be forgotten in which the Believers have no escape and the unbelievers are not punished! This is so that the Believers — the callers toward God — should remain fully aware that they can also meet this extreme end in the way of God, and they have no say in it. Their matter and the matter of belief rests with God.

Their task is to fulfill their obligation, and go. Their obligation is to choose God, prefer belief over life, raise themselves above persecution through faith, and to testify to God with deed as well as intention. Then it is up to God to deal with them and with their enemies, with His Religion and Call, as He deems proper. He may choose for them any one of the endings known in history, or some other ending which only He knows and sees.

They are workers for God. Whenever, whatever, however He wants them to do their work, they should do it and take the known reward. To decide what will be the ending of their endeavor is neither in their power nor is it their responsibility. This is the responsibility of the One in authority, not of those who are mere workers.

They receive the first part of their reward in the form of contentment of heart, height of understanding, beauty of ideas, liberation from desires and attractions, and freedom from fear and sorrow, in whatever condition they may be.

They receive the second part of their reward in praise, remembrance and honour among the angels, in addition to these among the people of this earth.

Then they receive the greater and the last part of their reward in the Hereafter: easy accounting and great favours.

With every kind of reward, they also receive the greatest of rewards: the pleasure of God. It is His bounty on them that He chose them for His purpose, an instrument for His power, so that He makes use of them on this earth as He deems proper.

* * *

The Qur'anic training of the first noble generation of Muslims was of this character to the highest degree. They lost their personalities and identities in this matter, acting as workers for the One in authority, and were pleased with God in every decision and in every condition. The training by the Prophet — peace be on him — went side by side with the Qur'anic teachings, turning their hearts and eyes toward the Garden, and toward patiently persevering in their assigned task until God ordains what He intends in this world as well as what is pleasing to Him in the Hereafter.

The Prophet — peace be on him — saw the intensity of tortures heaped upon 'Ammar, his father and his mother — may God be pleased with them — but he said nothing more than this: "Patience, family of Yasir! The Garden is promised for you."

And Khabbab bin al-Aratt — may God be pleased with him — reported: "We complained to the Messenger of God — peace be upon him — while he was resting in the shadow of Ka'aba, saying, 'Why do you not ask God to help us? Why do you not pray for us? Then he said: 'Before you, there were people who would catch a man, bury him halfway in a hole dug in the ground, then saw his head until it split in two; or would comb with iron combs between his flesh and bones; yet this would not turn him away from his religion. By God! God will bring this matter to completion, and a time will come when a rider will ride alone from San'a to Hadramut and he will have no fear except of God, or of a wolf against his sheep; but you people are in a hurry". (Bukhari)

* * *

God's wisdom underlies every decision and every condition. He administers the entire universe, and, He is informed of its beginning and its end, controlling its events and its inter-relationships. He knows the wisdom, hidden from us behind the curtains of the Unseen — the wisdom which, in conjunction with His will, unfolds the long process of history.

Sometimes, after generations and centuries, God unveils to us the wisdom of an event which was not understood by the contemporary people. They might have wondered: Why this? O Lord! Why did this happen? The question itself is due to ignorance from which the Believer saves himself. He already knows that behind every decision there is wisdom. His breath of concept and his far — seeing vision in space and time, and in values and scales, raises him above this unbelief whose beginning is in such a question. He journeys on God's ordained course with submission and contentment.

The Qur'an was creating hearts worthy of bearing the trust of being God's representatives on earth. It was necessary that these hearts be so solid, so strong and so pure, leaving behind everything and bearing everything patiently, as not to fix their sights on something of this earth, but looking beyond to the Hereafter, not seeking anything except the pleasure of God and being willing to traverse the path of life until death in poverty, difficulty, frustration, torment and sacrifice. They were not to seek any hasty reward on this earth, whether it was the reward of the victory of the Call, the dominance of Islam, and the glory of the Muslims, or even that this reward be the annihilation of the tyrants, as the All Mighty, the All Powerful had dealt with former generations of unbelievers. When such hearts were found which knew that during the course of this life they would have no expectations, and that the decision between the truth and falsehood would be made in the Hereafter — when such hearts were found, and God knew the sincerity of their intentions concerning which they had pledged, he gave them victory in the earth and bestowed upon them the trust. This trust was not for their benefit, but so that they might establish the Divine system.

They became the bearers of this trust when no promise was made to them of worldly benefits which they could have demanded, nor were their sights fixed on acquiring such benefits. They were dedicated servants of God from the day they knew of no reward except His pleasure.

All the verses of the Qur'an in which victory is promised, or in which spoils are mentioned or where it is told that the polytheists will be punished in this world by the hands of the Believers, were revealed in Medina. These were revealed only after all these matters were excluded from the Believer's scope of action, his expectation and his desire. God's help came on its own, when God intended that this way of life become actual in the life of mankind, so that generations of men could see it in a practical and concrete form, and not as a reward for the endeavors, the hard work, the sacrifice and the sufferings. This was indeed a decision of God, the wisdom of which we are trying to fathom today.

This intricate point requires deep thought by all callers toward God, to whatever country or period of time they belong; for this guarantees that they will be able to see the milestones of the road clearly and without ambiguity, and establishes the path for those who wish to traverse it to the end, whatever this end may be; then what God intends to do with His Call and with them is up to Him. Then they will not be anxious, while traversing this road ever paved with skulls and limbs and blood and sweat, to find help and victory, or desirous that the decision between the truth and falsehood be made on this earth. However, if God Himself intends to fulfill the completion of His call and His religion through their efforts, He will bring about His will — but not as a reward for their sufferings and sacrifices. Indeed, this world is not a place of reward.

* * *

Another fact to ponder here is a comment of the Qur'an on the story of the Makers of the Pit where God Most High says:

> ***"And they were angered with the Believers, only because they believed in God, the All — Powerful, the All — Praiseworthy."***

The callers to God, of any period or generation, ought to think over this deep truth.

The struggle between the Believers and their enemies is in essence a struggle of belief; and not in any way of anything else. The enemies are angered only because of their faith, enraged only because of their belief.

This was not a political or an economic or a racial struggle; had it been any of these, its settlement would have been easy, the solution of its difficulties would have been simple. But essentially it was a struggle between beliefs — either unbelief or faith, either ***Jahiliyyah*** or Islam.

This is why the leaders of the polytheists of Mecca offered the Messenger of God — peace be on him — wealth, kingship and worldly things against only one thing: that he give up the struggle of belief and settle with them in this affair. Had he accepted — may God forgive us for saying this — what they asked of him, no difference whatsoever would have remained between them and him.

Indeed, this was a question of belief and a battle of belief. The Believers ought to be certain of this, whatever be the declaration of their enemies. They are their enemies only because of their belief — "only because they believe in God, the All — Powerful, the All — Praiseworthy" — and because they purify for Him alone their obedience and submission.

The enemies of the Believers may wish to change this struggle into an economic or political or racial struggle, so that the Believers become confused concerning the true nature of the struggle and the flame of belief in their hearts becomes extinguished. The Believers must not be deceived, and must understand that this is a trick. The enemy, by changing . the nature of the struggle, intends to deprive them of their weapon of true victory, the victory which can take any form, be it the victory of the freedom of spirit as was case of the Believers in the story of the Maker of the Pit, or dominance in the world — as a consequence of the freedom of spirit — as happened in the case of the first generation of Muslims.

We see an example of this today in the attempts of Christendom to try to deceive us by distorting history and saying that the Crusades were a form of imperialism. The truth of the matter is that the latter — day imperialism is but a mask for the crusading spirit, since it is not possible for it to appear in its true form, as it was possible in the Middle Ages. The unveiled crusading spirit was smashed against the rock of the faith of Muslim leadership which came from various elements, including Salahuddin the Kurd and Turan Shah the Mamluk, who forgot the differences of nationalities and remembered their belief, and were victorious under the banner of Islam.

> ***"They were angered with the Believers only because they believed in God, the All — Powerful, the All — Praiseworthy."***

Almighty God spoke the truth, and these treacherous deceivers are liars!

* * *